SCATTERED TO
FOCUSED

SCATTERED TO
FOCUSED

Smart Strategies to
Improve Your Child's Executive
Functioning Skills

Zac Grisham, MS, LPC-S, ADHD-CCSP

**ROCKRIDGE
PRESS**

For general information on our other products and services or to obtain technical support, please contact our Customer Care Department within the United States at (866)
744-2665, or outside the United States at (510) 253-0500.

Rockridge Press publishes its books in a variety of electronic and print formats. Some
content that appears in print may not be available in electronic books, and vice versa.

Interior and Cover Designer: Tricia Jang
Art Producer: Samantha Ulban
Editor: Annie Choi
Production Editor: Rachel Taenzler

All images used under license Shutterstock. Author photo courtesy of Jennifer Dawn
Photography.

ISBN: Print 978-1-64739-677-0 | eBook 978-1-64739-416-5

R0

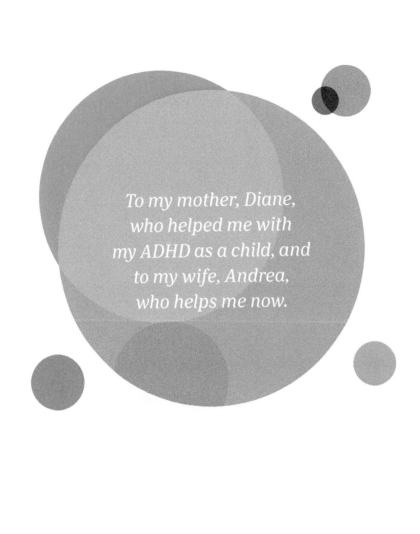

To my mother, Diane,
who helped me with
my ADHD as a child, and
to my wife, Andrea,
who helps me now.

CONTENTS

INTRODUCTION

In my counseling practice, I primarily work with children ages 5 to 14, many of them diagnosed with ADHD or another disorder that affects their attention and organization skills. It is like looking back in time to my own childhood, because I myself was diagnosed with ADHD at the age of 15.

Nearly 25 years later, I see many of the same patterns in the children I work with today, from trouble remembering which homework is due, to difficulty controlling impulses, to an inability to create or stick to new routines. I also see how these difficulties affect how children view themselves and the world. These challenges can lead to feelings of helplessness, a lack of confidence, and an internal conflict of wanting to change but not knowing how to do it.

The good news is there are many research-based strategies that can help. Through my own personal journey with ADHD and by coaching countless children, I've learned that parents can make a huge difference in boosting their children's executive functioning skills, which are mental skills that help us do things like focus, regulate our emotions, and plan ahead, to name a few.

Who Should Read This Book?

This book is written for the parents of children between the ages of 4 and 12. You may have a diagnosis or a simple suspicion that your child has ADHD or other executive functioning issues. These children are typically very intelligent, but are often confusing to their parents. For example, they may have talents in some areas of their life and significant difficulty in other areas. They may be able to focus for hours on building blocks, but drift off after four minutes while trying to do homework. They may get extremely frustrated about something that seems very insignificant. They may have very high IQ scores, but make low grades at school. They may continue to make the same mistakes, despite numerous discussions about their actions. They may frustrate parents because they seem to get distracted when given seemingly simple instructions. They may procrastinate and even be called "lazy," but have an unlimited amount of passion and energy for the things that interest them.

It's my hope that this book will help parents of these children, not just by giving tips to discipline or motivate their children with executive functioning challenges, but also to teach them ways to build the skills that may be lagging. The intention here is to build on these lagging skills with the child's self-esteem in mind. Many children with ADHD or executive functioning difficulties lack resilience or self-esteem, and may seem easily discouraged. Oftentimes this happens because they are being punished for their disability by people who don't understand the reason behind the behavior and treat the behavior as laziness, disregard, or selfishness. In this book, parents will get recommendations that will seek to help their child feel more confident, validated, and in control of their world.

This book is not just for children with a formal diagnosis of ADHD or disorders affecting executive functioning skills. The recommendations in this book can help any child build upon their executive functioning skills, whether they have an official diagnosis or not. These relatable and simple ideas can help enhance growth in the executive functioning of any child.

Why This Book?

This book is written by someone who has firsthand understanding of the mind of a child with ADHD. Every strategy and recommendation you'll find in this book is based on both lived experience and years of private practice counseling kids with attention difficulties. The tools and strategies take into account the unique strengths and weaknesses of children with attention-related learning differences.

This book will shed light on some of the difficulties that parents of children with ADHD and executive functioning disorders regularly face. It will also help you assess your child's executive functioning skills, as well as yours, so you can become more empathetic and aware.

All the ideas in this book are based on research but explained without the jargon. The tools and strategies are organized by specific skill to make them ready to use. The structure also makes this book easy to navigate when you need to revisit a specific strategy in the moment.

Many of these strategies will work at home, but there are also ideas that could help in the school environment. Several strategies are based on my experience collaborating with teachers and administrators to develop accommodation plans for children with attention issues, as well as my own experience as an elementary school teacher.

What You'll Learn

This book has two parts. In part 1 (chapters 1 to 3), you'll learn what you need to know about ADHD and executive functioning deficits, how to assess your own executive functioning skills as parents, and how to determine your child's executive functioning strengths and weaknesses.

Part 2 (chapters 4 to 10) will dive into the strategies. Each chapter is devoted to a specific executive functioning skill, including practicing self-control, regulating emotions, boosting memory, creating and following routines, staying focused in the classroom, time management, and resilience.

In each chapter of part 2, you will start by learning general coaching strategies to help your child build the specific executive functioning skill. Following these general strategies, you'll get in-the-moment strategies to help with problematic issues that stem from that particular executive functioning weakness. You'll also get ideas for providing support in the school environment, common pitfalls to avoid, and fun ways to work on the specific executive functioning skill at home. Each chapter ends with a personal tip from someone with ADHD—me!

You Can Make a Difference

Being a parent of a child with executive functioning deficits can be difficult. It takes so much more out of you as a parent, especially if you don't have a learning or thinking difference yourself. It can even be tempting to label your child as lazy, selfish, or irresponsible.

Here is a statistic to help put your feelings into perspective: Up to 40 to 50 percent of children with an ADHD diagnosis will not exhibit ADHD symptoms as adults. The gaps that you may now see between your child and their peers can and often do close.

But for now, it's important to have honest and realistic expectations for your child. Instead of expecting them to do what they can't because they lack certain skills, think about what you *can* teach your child. This book will help you focus on developing those skills and preparing your child for adulthood, while simultaneously building their confidence and resilience in time. So many of these children go on to excel, becoming professors, athletes, writers, musicians, entrepreneurs, actors, business leaders, and experts in their field, but they need your help to get there.

PART ONE

Understanding Executive Function

Part 1 covers what you need to know as parents with children who struggle with executive functioning skills. In chapter 1, we'll explore what executive functioning is and how it develops in children. We'll also discuss common myths about children with ADHD and executive functioning deficits, as well as some of the maladaptive patterns of thinking that affect their self-esteem and family dynamics. Chapter 2 will help you assess your own strengths and weaknesses with executive functioning in order to understand their potential effects on your parenting style. Once you understand what you bring to the table, you'll use chapter 3 to assess your child's executive functioning deficits.

CHAPTER
ONE

What Parents
Need to Know

The best part about understanding your child's executive functioning skills is that you can then adapt your parenting style to your child's needs. This chapter will help you challenge some of the myths and maybe even some of your own assumptions about children with ADHD. When you understand how a potential lack of development of your children shows in their behavior, you can better empathize with their struggles and reduce unnecessary conflict.

What Is Executive Functioning?

Executive functioning skills are neurologically based skills that help us rise above our instinct and make smart decisions for the long term, not just what's desirable in the moment. This is what separates Dr. Bruce Banner from the Hulk in the comic books and movies! These skills originate primarily in the prefrontal cortex of our brain, which is one of the last parts of the brain to develop. For most people, the prefrontal cortex doesn't fully develop until their mid- to late 20s. This is one reason that ADHD affects children more than adults; in fact, people diagnosed with ADHD may be as much as 30 percent delayed in the development of their executive functioning skills.

Some life skills that stem from executive functioning include:

→ Self-control
→ Emotional regulation
→ Working memory
→ Ability to stick to routines
→ Sustained focus
→ Time management
→ Resilience

Let's explore how each of these areas can present a struggle for the child with ADHD.

Self-Control

One of the most important executive functioning skills is the ability to practice self-control. A great example of the importance of developing self-control in children is the

"Marshmallow Test" conducted by Walter Mischel in the 1960s and 1970s. In this test, a child was brought into a room and presented with a marshmallow. The child was told that the adult had to leave the room, but if they could keep from eating the marshmallow until the adult returned, the child would get two marshmallows instead of just the one they were presented with. If they couldn't wait, they wouldn't get the extra bite of fluffy deliciousness. The adult would then leave the room for 15 to 20 minutes, or until the child could no longer resist eating the marshmallow in front of them, whichever came first.

Years later, Mischel and the researchers followed up with some of the participants. They found that the children who were able to wait successfully or delay gratification displayed higher scores on cognitive testing and SATs, as well as a stronger ability to cope with frustration.

If you think about it, being an adult is like one big Marshmallow Test. We wait for our paychecks, the weekend, or our vacation. Life requires constant waiting and patience. This ability to delay gratification is a core executive functioning skill. Most children with ADHD do not truly begin to show mature self-control until their junior year of high school.

The good news, however, is that you can help strengthen your child's self-control, as you'll learn in chapter 4 (see page 63).

Emotional Regulation

Emotional regulation is another core executive functioning skill that's tough to master, even for adults. So many children I work with are drawn to the Hulk, probably because they relate to his ability to let go and express strong emotions with no visible consequences.

The ability to manage our emotions, however, keeps us employed, allows us to develop and maintain relationships, and keeps us safe overall. People with ADHD or executive functioning deficits are often impulsive with their actions as well as their emotions. They have a hard time inhibiting their emotional response, so they may resort to making exaggerated remarks like, "I wish I was dead!" or "I wish I had different parents!" They may have difficulty remembering self-calming routines in the moment.

Here's a general timeline of how emotional regulation typically develops in children, according to research:

PRESCHOOL AGE – Child uses words to describe complex feelings and motivations.

ELEMENTARY SCHOOL AGE – Child understands social norms of how and when to express undesired emotions.

MIDDLE SCHOOL AGE – Child understands complex differences of when, where, how, and to whom they can appropriately express their emotions.

Children with ADHD or executive functioning deficits can be delayed in mastering their emotional regulation skills. Chapter 5 (see page 79) will explore how you can help develop these skills.

Working Memory

Boosting memory or adapting for memory delays is also very important. Without the ability to remember, we can't retain information necessary to learn. The child with a delayed working memory is more likely to repeat the same patterns of behavior over and over again. They may continually lose papers for class, struggle with writing, forget plans with friends, or have to repeat work over and over again.

Working memory is foundational to all learning and executive skills. In developmentally typical children, working memory is developed enough by age 6 to engage in complex tasks like following multi-step directions, according to research.

Children with ADHD or executive functioning deficits are often delayed in this area. When they are asked to engage in multi-step tasks that they are not ready for, they may lose focus, avoid tasks, or act out emotionally. Although it's fairly easy to help children with task-specific memory skills, it's more difficult to develop a stronger overall sense of working memory in children. You'll learn how to boost your child's working memory in chapter 6 (see page 101).

Following Routines

Many people with executive functioning weaknesses have a tough time creating and following routines; however, it's absolutely a key part of success for people with ADHD or executive functioning deficits.

Developing and following routines takes planning ahead. It requires setting a future goal and doing what's necessary today to reach that goal. Children with ADHD have difficulty with this, according to a 2017 study. For example, 4- and 5-year-olds with ADHD may only plan ahead up to 20 minutes. It may take a child with ADHD until he's 12 years old to be able to plan up to two to three days ahead in advance to reach a goal. And even 23- to 25-year-olds with ADHD may only be able to plan ahead three to five weeks to reach a goal.

This inability to plan ahead can affect their ability to create new routines in their life. In chapter 7 (see page 117), you will learn how to help establish routines and teach your child to plan ahead.

Sustained Focus

Although working memory sets the foundation for learning, all learning requires the ability to focus and pay attention. Many children with ADHD leave the classroom having retained only a portion of the lesson in the working memory part of their brain. Children with ADHD or executive functioning weaknesses often have to spend extra time and effort filling in the gaps because their ability to focus and receive information isn't developed. Kids can learn how to improve their sustained focus through self-awareness techniques, which we'll explore in chapter 8 (see page 131).

Kids with ADHD are told to "just focus" in the classroom. This is almost like telling a running back with a torn ACL to "just get up and play." They may be able to do it, but it would be really difficult and painful. The better way is for experts, like trainers, doctors, and nurses, to help the injured player get to the point where they can walk and run like everyone else.

As parents, we can be that trainer—so much better than someone on the sideline yelling at them to play! With improved working memory, people with ADHD can feel more competent and in control of their lives.

Time Management

Time management is tricky for those of us with ADHD or executive functioning deficits. It seems like time is constantly moving too fast or way too slow. Our internal clock is always a little off, like one of those cheap watches you might find at a souvenir shop.

However, like every other skill mentioned, time management skills can be strengthened. In chapter 9 (see page 147), you'll learn how to teach your child to use time management tools to meet expectations in school, as well as to manage social relationships and stress.

Resilience

Perhaps the most important skill that supports the development of all of the previously mentioned skills is resilience: the ability to adapt and overcome difficulties in your life. This is the number-one character trait that I'd like my children to have, because life is filled with adversity, and being able to adapt quickly and solve problems as they come at you can lead to a greater sense of confidence and self-esteem.

Unfortunately, children with ADHD and executive functioning deficits will have more opportunities to face challenges on a daily basis, so developing a resilient mindset can help these children deal with difficulties, so they can learn more quickly and adapt new strategies to solve daily problems.

Resilience is developed through mindset and self-talk. You can teach kids to observe their productive and unproductive thoughts and stick with productive ones. For children with ADHD, it's not really natural to slow down to think about their thoughts or contemplate whether to give up or stick it out when the going gets tough, but with a little awareness of what works best, you can help develop this skill in your child with the tools in chapter 10 (see page 163).

Rethinking Our Approach

Executive functioning weaknesses can create a gap between potential and performance, and this can negatively affect a child's self-esteem and how they see the world. People with ADHD often feel scattered and out of control, like they're constantly treading water in a strong current at the mercy of the sea. This feeling, combined with being surrounded by people who don't understand or empathize with their struggles, can have an adverse effect on a child's self-esteem.

When children live and learn in environments with constant negative feedback and little understanding of their strengths and weaknesses, it can lead to really scary ways of thinking. For example, many children I work with in my counseling practice say things like, "I can't control myself," "Everyone is always angry at me," or "I'm just a bad kid."

I also see children who become extremely anxious because they are so nervous about making mistakes and getting reprimanded after years of being told "Stop!" and "Why do you always do this?" They assume people are annoyed with them even when they are not. This anxiety can lead to over-apologizing, feeling worried about making mistakes, and thinking that their mistakes are a much bigger deal than they actually are.

It's sad to think about a child feeling so down on themselves for something that's out of their control. But you are here with this book because you care and you want your child to not just flourish academically and socially, but also to feel good inside about the awesome kid they are and the potential that they have. With a better understanding of where they're coming from, parents can increase their awareness and learn healthier patterns of relating and responding.

Underdeveloped Skills

Many parents of children with executive functioning weaknesses complain about their child's inability to take responsibility for their actions as if the child has a choice—oftentimes they do not. This pattern of complaining about a child's lack of responsibility leads to resentment, avoidance, and lack of resilience. The child is made to feel powerless, as they begin to label themselves as lazy or irresponsible, thinking that this is just who they are, so they can't recover. To the parent this lack of accountability may seem like a willful act, but it is most often a symptom of underdeveloped working memory and need for other stimulation such as skill-building and positive reinforcement. In order for a child to be able to take responsibility for their actions, they must be able to:

→ Control their impulses
→ Evaluate a social situation
→ Understand other people's points of view
→ Problem-solve effectively

These are all skills that may be underdeveloped with children with ADHD or executive functioning issues.

Children with ADHD or executive functioning weaknesses don't learn appropriate accountability at a young age, because their underdeveloped executive functioning causes them to move on from a conflict without fully understanding the consequences of their actions. For example, after a conflict with a parent, they may say that they wished their parents were dead and then ask them to make them pancakes for breakfast five minutes later. They don't take the time to think about their actions and feel guilty in that moment, so they often move on and avoid undesirable emotions altogether. This may lead to personalization or the blame game. For example, the child with ADHD often thinks that negative consequences are all their fault and that they're a bad person, or conversely, that the undesired consequence wasn't their fault at all and they shouldn't have to make up for it. This seesaw effect can be frustrating for parents. They may themselves internally go back and forth between thinking that they are being either too hard or too easy on their child. And those conflicting thoughts make it difficult to parent consistently.

As parents, it's your job to be the calm in the storm but also to give your child an opportunity to slow down and think so they can feel the appropriate emotional consequences. Doing so can help motivate them to behave differently in the future. This may be a short redirection to ask them to think about what just happened and the effect on the family, and why they did what they did. It may involve a calm and non-judgmental talk later in the day addressing the undesired behavior, so the child can feel guilt in a safe way that they can't automatically avoid.

Effect on Family Relationships

Let's just admit it: ADHD is hard to understand for the average parent. As a kid, I could list off the batting averages for the 1989 Oakland Athletics, but I could never tell you where I left my backpack! The disparity in performance is confusing and can lead to frustration fueled by misunderstandings over things like the contrast between a burst of intense focus on video games, dinosaur books, or building blocks and the struggle to complete a single homework problem. This lack of understanding by parents can wreak havoc on the entire family dynamic.

When parents assume their child doesn't care or is intentionally not performing, it can lead to resentment on the parents' side. This, in turn, causes avoidance in children since the parent is consistently upset about something that the child sees as out of their control. Avoidance may look like not caring about the parents' feelings or not trying to do something to solve the problem. The child may just dive into something interesting to them to not think about their parents' resentment. This avoidance often leads to a harmful dynamic that Edward Hallowell and John Ratey mention in their book *Driven to Distraction*. This book uses the relationship between spouses as an example, but it is something I commonly see with parents and children in my practice.

Avoidance starts with the child's ADHD symptoms of forgetfulness, disorganization, and distractibility that irritate parents due to a lack of understanding. The parent displays their frustration in a way that confuses and generally labels the child without understanding. The child then withdraws from the parent and doesn't ask for help with any executive functioning skills, which they absolutely need. The parent reiterates expectations, usually in a louder and more aggressive way, and then the child continues to display the same symptoms, leading to more resentment from the parent toward the child.

It's a dangerous cycle, and the responsibility is on the parents to break that cycle. Breaking this pattern requires education, patience, empathetic discussions of expectations, and an accurate understanding of ADHD or executive functioning deficiencies.

Although that may sound a bit overwhelming, picking up this book is a great first step. Studies have shown that parental understanding of ADHD is the number-one predictor of adult success for children with ADHD.

Inconsistent Performance

In elementary and middle school, I was in the gifted and talented program. I also loved sports, and played basketball, baseball, and soccer. When I saw the attention that the junior high football players got from cheerleaders, teachers, and the like, I wanted to be a part of this, so in eighth grade I joined the football team.

After the first practice, I was thrown in as quarterback because the coach saw me pitch well in a local baseball tournament and thought I had potential. But I had no idea how to call a play in the huddle, nor of the difference between an X or a Y receiver, and I generally felt clueless. I could not pick up or understand the basics of the game due to my difficulty learning new concepts as a result of a poor working memory. When I called the wrong play during a game, the coach called me over and grabbed me by the facemask and yelled, "You're the dumbest smart kid I've ever seen!"

Looking back, this comment encapsulates the treatment and the conflicting messages I received growing up, and this is probably common for those kids who have much potential—when they don't meet expectations, the feedback from adults can be overwhelmingly negative. Adults just cannot understand how someone with strong test scores could forget to bring a pencil to class. In my case, this lack of understanding led me to believe that my brain just did not work right and that I was personally defective.

It's critical that parents or adults working with children with ADHD or executive functioning issues understand the internal frustration of these children. The way we react is critical in preventing the development of some of these damaging beliefs.

Assuming Negative Intent

A big issue that I see in school conference meetings stems from the school's misunderstanding of the nature of ADHD and misinterpretation of intent. Too often, teachers speak as if the child is defiantly not paying attention or that they have a character flaw. For example, if the child forgets their homework, they may be called lazy or uncaring.

In reality, the majority of the children that I work with spend more time on their homework than their peers and are more tired at the end of the day. This is because they are using up more mental energy trying to attend and focus in an unstimulating environment, or an environment that demands focus and attention on subjects that aren't exciting to them.

When adults assume negative intent, the effect is extremely damaging to the child's self-esteem. So often, children are given negative feedback for something they can't control, because adults think that they are trying to get away with something on purpose. This is like saying to a child who's going to their first swim lesson, "I'm going to take away your favorite toy if you can't swim across the pool." They'll immediately feel powerless and out of control.

It's vital that parents use negative reinforcement with children with ADHD or executive functioning deficits only at appropriate times; that is, if the child already has a grasp on the skill needed.

As an adult parenting or working with a child with ADHD, it's important to challenge any assumptions that get in the way of really helping them. The misinterpretation of intent is an example of one such myth—that people with ADHD or executive functioning weaknesses are simply lazy, which is not true. Here are some other common myths about ADHD:

People with ADHD or executive functioning deficits cannot focus on anything.

False. If you have a child with ADHD, you know that they can spend hours and hours building things or practicing their baseball swing outside. This ability to hyperfocus—to dive into a project and go all in—is a strength for many children and adults with ADHD. ADHD is less about the inability to focus. Rather, it's the inability to *regulate* focus and attention, causing them to focus either too much or not enough.

ADHD/executive functioning weaknesses only affect a child's academic life.

False. The more I learned about ADHD as an adult, the more I saw that it affected every facet of my life, from relationships, to self-esteem, to behavioral issues, and so on.

Children with ADHD need a completely rigid and structured parent.

False. Although routines and structure are important, an inflexible parenting approach can be very damaging to a child with ADHD or executive functioning issues. Conversely, flexibility and creativity within a structured environment can pave the way to an ideal environment for healthy growth (more on this in chapter 7, page 117).

ADHD is caused by parental style.

False. Highly influenced by genetics, ADHD is in fact one of the most heritable diagnoses. Although environmental factors such as poor diet or stressful home life can exacerbate symptoms of ADHD, it does not cause ADHD.

ADHD medications can lead to addiction in adulthood.

False. There is no evidence that stimulant medication in childhood leads to substance abuse as an adult.

ADHD is not a serious mental health issue.

False. Children with untreated ADHD are twice as likely to die in childhood. Untreated ADHD reduces the average American life span about 13 years compared to treated ADHD, due to increased rates of accidents requiring emergency room visits, depression, impulse control, and unhealthy lifestyles such as addiction, overeating, overwork, or other excesses. In fact, ADHD is a public health issue, affecting a broader scope of society than just the individual. Fortunately, things like treatment, skill-building, positive role models and reinforcement, empathy, therapy, and medication monitoring can all greatly influence the rate of success, as can a parent's understanding of what an ADHD diagnosis truly is.

People with ADHD are good at multitasking.

False. Interestingly, though we may not be good at multitasking two complex activities, or activities that require focus and attention, we do benefit from engaging in an activity that is simple and second nature to us while we are learning. This is why many schools allow the use of fidget gadgets in classrooms or bouncy balls to sit on.

Parents with executive functioning strengths can easily teach their children with executive functioning deficits.

False. Because people with strengths in the area of executive functioning were born with innate abilities, they rarely had to work on developing them. If you were born just knowing how to do something, it's not easy teaching how to do it to someone who doesn't understand it.

Children with ADHD need constant praise.

False. Children with ADHD need to see themselves as competent and able to manage their world. Encouraging their effort and process of getting desired results will help them repeat that performance much more effectively than will constant unearned words of praise.

ADHD is only treated with medication.

False. While many studies do show the efficacy of different types of medications in the treatment of ADHD, most studies show that a combination of an accurate diagnostic assessment, psychoeducation for parents and children, medication, accommodations for school and home use, and behavior modification or therapy is most effective.

Children with ADHD or executive functioning deficits are selfish.

False. So many of the children I work with may not apologize or readily engage with their family. They may also have difficulty sharing, or may consistently bring the topic of conversation back to what they want. But they may also be the ones who will stop the car to make sure their mom and dad pick up the stray cat so they can find its home, or they may want to see pictures of a loved one's baby. Children with ADHD often fluctuate between seeming self-concerned and extremely empathetic. This is not a character flaw, but rather a result of underdeveloped social thinking.

I hope that you were able to gain a deeper understanding of what ADHD and executive functioning skills involve. Here are the key takeaways:

→ Parents can best benefit their child by educating themselves and adapting their parenting style to accommodate their child's strengths and areas of desired growth.

→ The goal is to help develop the executive functioning skills your child will need as an independent adult, while building and preserving their sense of self-esteem and capabilities.

→ As your understanding grows, you'll have a newfound acceptance and empathy of your child's situation. You'll know them better, and as a result, you won't expect them to be what they're not.

In the next chapter, we'll talk about assessing your own executive functioning skills and explore how your strengths and weaknesses affect your style of parenting.

Assess Your Own Executive Functioning

Not surprisingly, what parents bring to the table has a profound effect on the children they are raising. This is especially true for parents of children with ADHD or executive functioning deficits. Whether you yourself have a diagnosis of ADHD or not, this chapter will help you understand how your own executive functioning skills affect your parenting style, and how you can take this knowledge to become a more adaptive parent.

This chapter will focus on the influence of certain parenting styles on children with ADHD or executive functioning issues and includes a self-assessment of your own executive functioning skills as a parent, as well as an explanation of how those specific skills (or lack thereof) in parents affect children with ADHD and executive functioning deficits.

Parental Influence

Although genetics drives how ADHD presents itself in children, parenting style and parents' own executive functioning skills do affect children's ADHD symptoms and executive functioning. In fact, a parent's own ADHD symptoms can exacerbate ADHD symptoms in children. The good news, according to a recent study, is that parental involvement and understanding of ADHD helps moderate some ADHD symptoms in children.

In my counseling practice, I've noticed that many parents with children who have ADHD tend to be more punitive and anxious. This is understandable. Constantly needing to remind and redirect kids can be frustrating and exhausting for parents. Other parents go the opposite direction and become overly compliant. These parents seem almost too tired to give the consistent feedback that children with ADHD need. Another study shows that inconsistent feedback can negatively affect the development of executive functioning skills.

Parents who have their own ADHD symptoms often provide inconsistent discipline. Parents who give inconsistent discipline do not cause ADHD symptoms in children, but this inconsistency can lead to a less-than-optimal environment to address the development of executive functioning skills. This loop of sorts, of the parent's ADHD symptoms affecting the children's ADHD symptoms, can lead to resentment on both sides of the relationship. That's why it is extremely important for parents to evaluate their own executive functioning skills and subsequently adapt their environment and parenting style to address their own strengths and weaknesses so they can help their children develop and grow in their executive functioning skills.

Parenting Styles

The three common parenting styles are authoritarian, permissive, and authoritative. The authoritarian parent has high expectations on performance but shows little attention to the emotional state of the child. The permissive parent is the opposite. This parent displays high empathy and positive feedback but has very few expectations and sets inconsistent boundaries for the limits that they do have.

The most effective parenting style is authoritative. An authoritative parent is in control of themselves and their emotions but does not need control or expect complete compliance from the child. This parent has high expectations and sets clear limits, but also provides significant positive emotional feedback. This style is most effective because it promotes a secure attachment between the child and parent, which in turn enables the child to explore secure attachments with other people outside their immediate family. An authoritative approach to parenting can help decrease anxiety and aggression, increase resilience, and assist with the development of problem-solving skills, because these children feel secure in being able to make mistakes and know where social boundaries are.

If you see yourself as more authoritarian or permissive, my hope is that this chapter and this book will help you adopt a more authoritative parental style. This is not meant to criticize your parenting ability, since we are all growing as parents. We are all programmed a certain way, whether biologically or environmentally. But true growth comes from transcending that programming, and the first step is being aware of our own limitations and strengths as a parent.

Here's a short questionnaire to help you learn a little bit more about your executive functioning skills. (This questionnaire is not diagnostic in nature.)

RATE EACH STATEMENT TO THE BEST OF YOUR ABILITY.

1	2	3	4	5
Strongly Disagree	Disagree	Not Sure/ Neutral	Agree	Strongly Agree

SECTION 1: SELF-CONTROL

1. It's difficult for me to control my urges. _____
2. I am known to interrupt people. _____
3. I often say things that I regret. _____
4. I often make decisions on the spur of the moment. _____

Total: _____

SECTION 2: EMOTIONAL REGULATION

1. I often get into arguments. _____
2. My relationships have suffered due to my inability to control my emotions. _____
3. I have a hard time separating my emotions in a work-place setting. _____
4. When I experience a strong feeling, I find it hard to focus on a task at hand. _____

Total: _____

SECTION 3: WORKING MEMORY

1. I often forget where important items are. _____
2. I often have trouble remembering names. _____
3. Other people often seem to think more quickly than I do. _____
4. I often need reminders to finish important tasks. _____

Total: _____

SECTION 4: FOLLOWING ROUTINES

1. I have difficulty with long-term projects. _____
2. I often feel like I have a lack of purpose. _____
3. I often find myself stuck in life. _____
4. I have difficulty setting and achieving goals. _____

Total: _____

SECTION 5: FOCUS AND ATTENTION

1. I often take longer to produce work than my peers. _____
2. I often start and stop work many times. _____
3. I notice many times that I drift off and miss important communication in work meetings. _____
4. I have difficulty sitting through lectures that aren't interesting to me and learning something with ease. _____

Total: _____

continued →

SECTION 6: TIME MANAGEMENT

1. I rarely feel like I have enough time in the day to get everything done. _____
2. I often procrastinate and finish big projects at the last minute. _____
3. I am often late for appointments or social gatherings. _____
4. I'm not good at estimating the amount of time an activity takes. _____

Total: _____

SECTION 7: RESILIENCE

1. I find it difficult to respond after negative feedback. _____
2. I often can't get negative thoughts out of my head. _____
3. I do not respond well to pressure. _____
4. I have difficulty changing plans without frustration. _____

Total: _____

What Does This Mean for You?

The lowest scores indicate an area of strength in that particular skill, and the highest scores show an area of weakness in that particular skill. For example, if you got a score of 8 in section 1: Self-Control and a score of 14 for section 6: Time Management, your ability to practice self-control may be stronger than your ability to manage time effectively.

Now that you have a basic understanding of where you stand, let's look at how a particular area of weakness may affect you as a parent. Then we'll explore how to work with your unique skill sets to help your child with ADHD or executive functioning issues.

Improving Your Self-Control

If you struggle with practicing self-control, I'm right there with you! It's not easy to practice self-control when you see that new car you want to buy, or see the dessert tray being rolled out through a restaurant. There are too many awesome things in life, and it's easy to get carried away.

As mentioned earlier, a parent who struggles with self-control can have trouble giving the consistent feedback necessary to change behaviors in children. If the parent is impulsive at times, they may just give in to a whining 5-year-old who wants a toy at the grocery store. Impulsivity by parents can also lead to potential anxiety in children because they cannot consistently predict their parent's behavior or choices. This anxiety makes it difficult to learn new skills to improve their executive functioning deficits.

If you need to improve your self-control, it may be good for you to find an accountability partner. An accountability partner could be a spouse, co-parent, friend, therapist, spiritual or religious leader, or anyone, really, who has strong executive functioning skills. Make sure that you're comfortable enough with this person to be able to talk about your weakness and desire to grow in this area.

You and your accountability partner can have weekly coffee meetings or virtual chats, or just catch up through text, but the goal of these meetings would be to talk about recent successes and failures when it comes to practicing self-control as a parent of a child with executive functioning issues or ADHD.

→ Have you let some behavior go without giving feedback because you couldn't deal with it in the moment?
→ Have you given in impulsively to a screaming tantrum because you were tired?
→ Have you displayed consistency as a parent in the previous week?
→ Were there any moments in which you were particularly proud of your parenting choices?

You can discuss and process this with your accountability partner as a way of not just being accountable, but also helping you remember and keep these goals in mind.

Managing Your Emotions

Our emotions often guide our behavior in life. I find that when I am stressed, angry, or depressed, it's difficult for me to be the parent that I want to be. In my practice, the children whose parents display a lack of emotional regulation often express increased anxiety, depression, defiance, and lack of executive functioning skills. As you can imagine, these negative reactions are exacerbated in children with ADHD, as they have a greater need for behavioral reinforcement, reminders, and incentives. This instability can create more opportunities for frustration.

If you struggle with emotional regulation, you will likely benefit greatly from practicing stress management techniques. Some typical stress management techniques can include doing yoga or meditation, "unplugging" and putting down the phone for an extended period of time, making time for a hobby, or engaging in a good workout.

Perhaps more important, you'll want to examine the thoughts that lead to your emotional reactions. Some common disturbing thoughts are:

→ "What will my child be like when they're 25 if they can't get this mastered?"
→ "I'm an awful parent because I can't help them change."
→ "What's wrong with my child?"
→ "My kid will never fit in if he acts like this."

Ask yourself where those thoughts came from and how they developed. Take some time to wonder if these thoughts do you any good. Then consider if your reaction does anything to help the situation. More than likely, these thoughts and reactions just lead to more stress, make the child feel at fault, and prevent you from becoming that authoritative parent that you want to be.

When these thoughts persist, reframe your perspective. Remind yourself that 40 to 50 percent of children with an ADHD diagnosis will not exhibit symptoms as adults, as studies have shown. Remind yourself that some of the gaps that you see between your child with ADHD and neurotypical children will potentially close naturally with brain development, and even more so with your support and guidance. And remember that your child did not choose to have ADHD or executive functioning weaknesses. If you find yourself becoming angry or frustrated at your child's behavior, keep reading this book and other books about ADHD. As you build your understanding of their unique and very real journey, you'll find greater empathy for your child's struggles.

Remembering Parenting Goals

Parenting is hard, even for parents with strong working memory and processing speed. But if you struggle with executive functioning, parenting can feel doubly hard, adding more stress and pressure to your life that will typically spill over into your parenting approach.

Working memory is where I struggle the most, and it affects my ability to give consistent reinforcement and follow new parenting strategies, such as behavior plans. In my observation, parents who display ADHD symptoms have a tough time following my recommendations, not because they don't value the information, but because they just can't remember it all and put it into consistent practice. With these parents I may work with them more closely or recommend other treatment options for their ADHD symptoms.

Executive functioning is not about knowing what to do, but rather it is about doing what you know. The lapse in working memory affects your ability to get things done. For parents, it can lead to a much more passive parenting style with less structure.

I often recommend the use of technology, like phone apps, to help train your brain to remember important parenting goals. For example, if you consistently get a text reminding you daily of a parenting goal of having a simple time to talk with your daughter about her ability to focus in story time, sooner or later you are going to internally anticipate the text, and that will help you remember that goal so you can feel more organized, in control, and confident in supporting your child. We'll explore these kinds of strategies more deeply later in the book.

Modeling Good Routines and Habits

Trouble with working memory can also affect the ability to create and follow routines as parents. The two skills go hand in hand, as many of these executive functioning skills tend to overlap. But if you can create and follow routines, you'll be able to tackle more complex challenges in life and feel a greater sense of self-efficacy.

People with ADHD are often visual learners. If you have trouble creating and sticking to routines as a parent, you can use visual cues to remind yourself of your goals. A visual cue can be as simple as using your phone calendar to set up reminders for new parenting routines.

Sometimes, parents with ADHD or executive functioning deficits may have some internal resistance to change. This inflexibility can keep one stuck and prevent personal growth. It's important to identify and challenge negative thoughts that lead to this type of resistance.

It may be helpful to begin a nightly journal to reflect on your resistance to change for a week or two before enacting your new routine, so you don't have any conflicting thoughts that may inhibit you from creating new routines and following them. The nightly journal can also help you identify thoughts that could lead you to give up on the new routine.

As you journal, consider the following:

→ Does your goal feel impossible today because it has just been a bad day? If so, do you need a break or more support?

→ Is it that you cannot follow through because you have difficulty seeing how your efforts now will pay off in the future?

→ Is it just that you have trouble staying motivated to stick with your parenting goal because of your own executive functioning issues, like memory or emotional regulation?

A simple nightly reflection on these and other issues that come up for you can help you identify your blockers and help you push through when you get tempted to take the easy road.

Staying Focused

A lack of focus and attention can derail bonding with your children. When it's hard for you to stay focused while holding your baby, playing superheroes with your 5-year-old son, or listening to your teenage daughter who wants to tell you about her friends, you can miss out on big moments.

We may assume that those of us with difficulty focusing can naturally overcome deficits when it comes to our children because we love them. That is not always the case. This lack of focus does not mean we are less interested in them as a person or don't love them, but it's important to acknowledge that it's an area of needed growth so we can be more intentional in our interactions as parents.

One simple way to maintain focus is to know your limits. Focus for short and attainable amounts of time, and then see if you can do more. This approach may look like telling your child that you are going to play with them and set a timer. The playtime does not have to end with the buzzing of the timer, but at that point, you can relax your personal expectations of focus. As time goes on and you are able, you can increase the timer and try to maintain focus on your child and their play for longer amounts of time.

For older children, you may want to try to have conversations with them using the same idea. Start short and try to stretch yourself. Now, if you try to tell a 13-year-old, "Let's sit down and let me time this five-minute conversation," they'll look at you like they'd look at a flip phone—they'd have no use for you! So you'll have to be more subtle than that. Also, older kids may be a little more open to conversation in the car or while you're on a walk, where you're not directly facing each other. Start with some focused conversation, and then try to see if you can strengthen that focus muscle.

Modeling Time Management

Parents juggle so many responsibilities and expectations: longer work weeks, work demands after hours, parent-teacher conferences, time spent providing academic support for our children—the list goes on. It's easy to see how we struggle with time management with so much demanded of us.

But for a child, an inconsistent schedule and mismanaged time can lead to significant anxiety. Children with executive functioning issues often struggle with transitioning from one activity to another. If they are constantly pulled away to something new without warning, they will start to expect that they can be pulled away from an activity at a moment's notice. The anxiety that comes with not knowing what to expect can lead to issues with emotional regulation and a lack of focus.

I have found that being able to use alarms, voice reminders, and a calendar helps me anticipate time markers and makes my internal clock a little bit sharper. Once you can improve your own time management with technology, you can teach your child to do the same.

Becoming a Resilient Parent

The late Nelson Mandela, who displayed an enormous amount of resilience in his lifetime, once said, "Do not judge me by my successes, judge me by how many times that I fell down and got back up again." For parents raising children with ADHD or executive functioning weaknesses, cultivating resilience is vital for everyone involved.

It's important to maintain the belief that your child can and will grow despite the fact that they've forgotten where their backpack is for the 759th time, or you've caught them hiding cookies under their bed for the 125th time. Your child, and especially their brain, are still growing! The research strongly shows that they can close the gaps even if they're lacking certain skills right now.

Start each day reminding yourself that your goal is to help them reach adulthood as happy and healthy individuals, and not necessarily to solve all their problems that day. Have faith and believe in your child despite their struggles. Focus on developing their strengths and celebrate the small successes along the way. The less we allow a diagnosis or executive functioning weakness to define who they are as people, the less they will!

Sharing Your Results with Your Child

When you have more awareness about your own executive functioning strengths and weaknesses, you can strengthen your relationship with your children. In fact, the parents that I work with who are most aware of their own strengths and weaknesses are some of the most effective parents, because they can relate to their children.

Taking what you now know, start a conversation with your child about your own strengths and weaknesses as a parent. In my counseling sessions with children with ADHD, when I tell them that I was diagnosed with ADHD, their eyes light up and they exclaim, "Really?" So many children with executive functioning difficulties grow up thinking of themselves as damaged and feeling isolated. They feel such relief when they learn that their struggles do not mean that they are damaged, that there are so many successful people who overcame these struggles, and that they can grow in these areas. It can be extremely affirming to hear from someone, especially a parent, that you share some of their struggles and understand their experience, at least to some degree.

One way you can open a dialogue is to have the entire family fill out the questionnaires in this book (see pages 26 and 43) and discuss how each of your strengths and weaknesses have affected or currently affect your lives. It can help kids feel more understood if you share how your strengths and weaknesses affected you when you were their age.

Some parents worry that if their child knows that there is an executive functioning struggle at hand or if they have a diagnosis of ADHD, the child will use it as a crutch to avoid working hard, so the parent does not seek treatment for the child. However, oftentimes children with untreated ADHD who don't have knowledge of how their brain works can begin to feel out of control and unable to make progress like their peers, and those feelings can ultimately lead to a larger problem than using ADHD as a crutch, such as depression or issues with mood regulation. I encourage parents to have these personal conversations with their children, to normalize what they are going through and create opportunities to grow together.

Evaluate Your Child's Executive Functioning

In this chapter, you'll develop a deeper understanding of your child's executive functioning strengths and different areas of growth to help you pinpoint how best to support them. You'll fill out a questionnaire that can shed light on how to better understand your child's needs. You'll also learn the difference between intrinsic and extrinsic motivation, how executive functioning difficulties affect motivation, and how to help foster motivation in your children. Keep in mind that the questionnaires in this chapter are an educational tool and are not meant to diagnose or replace medical treatment.

Understanding Your Child's Strengths and Weaknesses

When I was around 15 years old, I had to do a big history project on Egypt. To help me avoid procrastination, my mom wrote up a contract that if I didn't start the project by a certain date, she would not take me to get any supplies needed for my presentation. I half-heartedly signed the contract and forgot about it.

When the final day for action approached, I blew my mom off, and so as promised, the night before the project was due, she would not take me to the store to get the supplies. After badgering my dad, he drove me to the store against my mother's wishes. I was up all night finishing the project, and it did not go well. When my Egyptian statue started falling apart during the verbal presentation, the class and the teacher started laughing. I then yelled at my teacher, who was eight months pregnant at the time. It was not my finest hour.

This anecdote illustrates the difficulties that a typical child with ADHD experiences: inability to get work started, last-minute planning, difficulty with prioritization, focus on immediate gratification (of not doing the project), and lack of emotional regulation.

It also speaks to my parents' conflicting views of the problem. My mom saw it as a lack of motivation and discipline, whereas my dad did not think it was a big deal. This was just one of many ways that my parents, either as a team or separately, tried to address my weaknesses in executive functioning. But neither of my loving and attentive parents understood how my brain worked or what underlying factors were contributing to the symptoms as well as they could.

Next, I'll help you get an accurate assessment of your children's strengths and weaknesses so you can build more effective strategies to address their needs.

Assessment Questionnaire

In chapter 2, you filled out a questionnaire about your own executive functioning skills (see page 26). In this questionnaire, you'll answer questions based on what you know about your child. This way, you can learn which executive functioning skills to focus on developing and which areas may be strengths that you can build upon. There are two different questionnaires: one for ages 4 to 7 and the other for ages 8 to 12, based on the developmental expectations of each age group.

RATE EACH STATEMENT TO THE BEST OF YOUR ABILITY.

1	2	3	4	5
Strongly Disagree	Disagree	Not Sure/ Neutral	Agree	Strongly Agree

QUESTIONNAIRE 1: AGES 4 TO 7

SECTION 1: SELF-CONTROL

1. My child has difficulty staying seated at the dinner table or in class. _____

continued →

2. My child has been known to have difficulty keeping her hands to herself. _____
3. My child has difficulty waiting to take a turn. _____
4. My child has difficulty staying quiet for more than a minute. _____

Total: _____

SECTION 2: EMOTIONAL REGULATION

1. My child often gets upset when he does not get his way. _____
2. My child is difficult to calm or soothe. _____
3. My child often threatens to hurt others. _____
4. My child has needed to leave social situations because of anger. _____

Total: _____

SECTION 3: BOOSTING MEMORY

1. My child often loses toys or other things important to her. _____
2. My child needs multiple reminders when asked to do something. _____
3. My child cannot remember his friends' names from school. _____
4. When learning something new, my child needs more repetition than other children her age. _____

Total: _____

1. My child needs consistent reminders to follow daily routines. _____

2. My child needs visual reminders for a bedtime or morning routine. _____

3. My child has difficulty adapting to new schedules like the start of school. _____

4. My child often has difficulty with two-step directions like, "Please go throw your trash away and go get your backpack." _____

Total: _____

1. My child has difficulty paying attention for more than a minute. _____

2. I consistently must repeat directions to my child. _____

3. I (or my child's teacher) have noticed that he seems to lose focus during verbal instruction after two to three minutes. _____

4. I notice that if I cannot give instructions or directions face-to-face with my child, she may not retain the information that I am giving. _____

Total: _____

1. My child can often start assignments but doesn't finish them. _____

continued →

2. My child often needs directions repeated to him. _____

3. My child often makes careless mistakes with homework or schoolwork. _____

4. My child's teacher often catches her daydreaming in the classroom. _____

Total: _____

SECTION 7: RESILIENCE

1. My child consistently complains when asked to do something mildly difficult. _____

2. I notice that my child takes disappointment harder than most children his age. _____

3. My child is extremely sensitive to any discipline I give her. _____

4. My child is not okay with making mistakes. _____

Total: _____

QUESTIONNAIRE 2: AGES 8 TO 12

SECTION 1: SELF-CONTROL

1. My child often speaks out of turn or interrupts other people during conversations. _____

2. My child has been known to have difficulty keeping his hands to himself. _____

3. My child does silly things to get other people's attention. _____

4. My child often says things without thinking. _____

Total: _____

SECTION 2: EMOTIONAL REGULATION

1. My child often gets upset when she does not get her way. _____
2. My child often yells when angry. _____
3. My child uses aggressive or mean language when angry. _____
4. My child's friends have avoided him on more than one occasion because of angry outbursts. _____

Total: _____

SECTION 3: WORKING MEMORY

1. My child often cannot tell me the events of the day at school. _____
2. My child has difficulty with following more than one direction at a time. _____
3. My child often forgets to bring materials home needed to do homework. _____
4. My child has difficulty recalling details when retelling a story. _____

Total: _____

SECTION 4: FOLLOWING ROUTINES

1. My child often seems unmotivated to follow daily routines. _____
2. My child needs visual reminders for a bedtime or morning routine. _____

continued →

3. My child has difficulty with long-term projects at school. _____

4. My child often says that she wants to do something better for herself, but can't follow through on practicing to improve in that area. _____

Total: _____

SECTION 5: TIME MANAGEMENT

1. My child has difficulty paying attention for 10 minutes on a subject that is not interesting to him. _____

2. I consistently must repeat directions to my child. _____

3. I (or my child's teacher) have noticed that she seems to lose focus during verbal instruction after two to three minutes. _____

4. I notice that if I cannot give instructions or directions face-to-face with my child, he may not retain the information that I am giving him. _____

Total: _____

SECTION 6: STAYING FOCUSED

1. My child often complains of losing focus when asked to stay seated for over 10 to 15 minutes. _____

2. My child is very avoidant of reading. _____

3. My child often brings work home that should have been finished in the classroom. _____

4. My child learns better in a hands-on manner rather than listening to a short tutorial or lecture about the subject. _____

Total: _____

1. My child consistently complains when asked to do something mildly difficult. _____

2. I notice that my child takes disappointment harder than most children her age. _____

3. My child is extremely sensitive to any discipline that I give him. _____

4. My child is not okay with making mistakes. _____

Total: _____

What Does It Mean for Your Child?

The lowest scores indicate a potential area of strength in that particular skill, and the highest scores show an area of weakness in a particular skill. For example, if your child's total score was an 8 in section 5: Time Management and 14 for section 6: Staying Focused, your child's ability to estimate and manage their time is probably stronger than their ability to maintain focus in the classroom. Use this questionnaire to help you determine where to focus your energy in the following chapters.

Understanding Motivation

Many parents of children with ADHD or executive functioning difficulties report having trouble motivating their children. They find their children extrinsically motivated, or only motivated by external things like rewards, prizes, or punishment.

It feels like they must be prodded, bribed, paid, or begged to accomplish tasks.

The constant need to provide extrinsic motivation for children is one of the most consistent challenges for the parents that I work with. The stress and mental exhaustion of having to use the carrot or the stick takes a toll on relationships.

In addition to being exhausting to enforce, extrinsic motivation is not sustainable for growth and learning. One study on motivation noted that when young children around the age of 5 years old who were already motivated to practice drawing were given a reward for practicing, their willingness to practice declined once the rewards were phased out. The children began to associate practicing drawing with the reward, not the act of learning or the pure enjoyment that comes from drawing.

Focusing on extrinsic motivation also ignores the actual needs of children with ADHD or executive functioning issues. One of the biggest reasons that those of us with attention issues seem extrinsically motivated is that the ability to motivate oneself is directly tied to executive functioning skills. If a child continually forgets something that motivates them, how can they be self-motivated? If a child cannot stick to a plan because of issues with impulse control, how can they build on their initial motivation to do something great? If they cannot follow through with routines, why don't they just give up on motivating themselves, because they're certain they will fail? This is the tricky thing about motivation with these kids—they may be motivated but lack the skills to follow through. They often depend on extrinsic motivation to get them through, but that doesn't solve the problem. Only skill-building will.

Now that we've explored extrinsic motivators and their pitfalls, we can focus on developing a child's intrinsic motivation, or the act of doing something without any need for external rewards. It creates a more sustainable solution that also reduces battles, the need for reminders, threats of punishment, or expensive rewards.

Motivation Questionnaire

Use this questionnaire to help you understand your child's current motivation level and determine whether your child is intrinsically motivated or not. Although young children can also be intrinsically motivated, this quick questionnaire focuses on evaluating children ages 9 to 12, who tend to have more demands placed on them.

RATE EACH STATEMENT TO THE BEST OF YOUR ABILITY.

1	2	3	4	5
Strongly Disagree	Disagree	Not Sure/ Neutral	Agree	Strongly Agree

1. My child will only do chores if promised a reward. _____
2. In a competitive environment, my child is overly focused on winning. _____
3. I feel like I constantly need to bribe or threaten my child. _____
4. My child consistently complains about typical daily tasks. _____

continued →

5. My child has difficulty with many daily tasks that she should have mastered. _____

6. Even when my child is engaging in a fun activity, he is consistently looking to something else that's more fun. _____

7. My child constantly asks for help with things that I know she can do for herself. _____

8. I notice that my child needs me around more than most children his age. _____

9. I feel like I'm constantly negotiating with my child. _____

10. My child has difficulty enjoying the little things in life. _____

11. My child is more focused on things rather than experiences. _____

12. My child seems preoccupied with social status more than most children her age. _____

Total: _____

→ If you scored a total of 50 or above, your child may be significantly extrinsically motivated.

→ If you scored between 35 and 50, your child may be moderately extrinsically motivated.

→ If you scored between 25 and 35, your child may be moderately intrinsically motivated.

→ If you scored under 25, your child may be significantly intrinsically motivated.

How to Encourage Intrinsic Motivation

So if your child seems extrinsically motivated, how can you help them become more intrinsically motivated? First, you'll need to understand the relationship between your child's motivation and their executive functioning weaknesses.

For example, let's say your child with ADHD or executive functioning difficulties seems motivated to learn to play the guitar because they think it would be enjoyable. This is awesome! They are displaying some intrinsic motivation, since they want to learn the skill simply for the value of learning a new skill.

But if your child has difficulty practicing self-control, they may impulsively skip a practice session to play video games with friends, and then tell themselves that since they skipped this time, they can skip more and more in the future. If your child displays a lack of emotional regulation, they may feel easily frustrated and irritated by learning new concepts and be more likely to give up. If they have difficulty remembering what motivates them, they may have difficulty sticking with their practice routine to get better at playing the guitar. If your child finds managing their time difficult, they may want to go practice enthusiastically, but then they realize 10 minutes into their practice session that dinner is ready, so they don't make much progress. And subsequently, if they can't display resilience in the face of the consistent failure of learning new things, they'll give up easily on the guitar. The more and more this pattern repeats, the less they'll engage in getting better at activities like learning the guitar, playing sports, or learning how to study by themselves. They'll give up because they don't see long-term growth as a possibility for them.

These executive functioning deficits are often perceived by adults as a lack of motivation. As parents, it is imperative to talk with these children about motivation. As you do, you'll want to keep these weaknesses that you've learned about in mind during this conversation. Of course, it's important to avoid using the word "lazy," because the child may start to use that label on themselves if they don't understand how their executive functioning issues affect their motivation.

Leading Discussions

In a 2016 study by Dr. Margaret Sibley, discussions based on motivational interviewing techniques were found to be effective for teens with ADHD. Her STAND (Supporting Teens' Autonomy Daily) treatment model relies heavily on parent involvement during therapy sessions to help the family understand the child's lack of motivation and instill intrinsic motivation in children with executive functioning difficulties.

To truly work on developing your child's intrinsic motivation, I encourage you to view it holistically and not as an individual failure in you or your child. If you can't access or aren't able to attend counseling sessions with a mental health professional trained in the STAND model, you can still have a discussion with your child using the STAND techniques.

This discussion should be a 10- to 15-minute weekly meeting to discuss long-term growth in regard to motivation. Some helpful goals of these discussions may be:

→ To help them understand the benefits of being self-motivated

→ For you to understand more about what motivates them, and see if they are willing to change without you pushing them with rewards or punishment

→ To help them feel validated enough to buy into the idea of changing and working on their motivation

→ To help with problem-solving skills and develop concrete plans to reach goals

Note that this is not meant to be a typical discussion about what they've done wrong or what you can do to motivate them.

Resolve Your Own Inner Conflict

As a parent wanting your child to change, you may be feeling some inner conflict. For example, perhaps you know deep down that doing most of your child's homework for them is robbing them of valuable learning opportunities, but you just don't want to deal with the constant complaining from your child or their failure to pass a class, so you maybe help them more than you know you should. Or you may be caught between giving your child a stern punishment and letting natural consequences take their course. Or you may be flip-flopping between the idea that your child's lack of motivation is all your fault and not your fault at all. No matter your particular struggle, have compassion for yourself and your child.

To address your child's lack of motivation, you'll want to have a clear vision and give consistent feedback, especially with children who haven't yet mastered executive functioning skills. This is a process involving education (like reading this book and completing the questionnaires) and reflection (like figuring out what your child needs and establishing the best ways to help them achieve that). It can be very beneficial to talk through challenges with other parents of children with executive functioning deficits or a therapist in order to develop a clear and consistent action plan for helping your child.

Ask Open-Ended Questions

When you discuss your child's lack of motivation with them, open-ended questions can be a great way to get insight. It also encourages more thought and sharing of ideas.

By open-ended, you're looking for them to provide an answer of their own, as opposed to a question that only requires an answer of "yes" or "no." One example may be "Tell me what you like about playing this game rather than starting your work." They may say, "I can just shut everything off when I play my video game and I don't have to worry about the world." If so, this tells you that one reason for their apparent lack of interest in schoolwork is anxiety, since they need a break from the world.

If they say, "I just don't think that I'm going to do well in this class," you can infer that their lack of self-confidence is affecting their motivation for school. If they say, "I hate having to do the same thing over and over again in school," issues with focus and attention may be the biggest factor. By asking questions in this way, you can gather helpful clues about your child's motivation.

Offer Affirming Responses

Everyone appreciates affirmations. Affirming responses recognize your child's strengths. These types of responses can lead to more open communication between you and your child.

An affirming response communicates acceptance and empathy in order to help your child feel safe enough to accept the challenge of improving themselves. These statements should not focus on the end results, but more on the process to get to the end result. They also reflect the feelings that your child is experiencing in those moments.

Affirming responses are also more specific than praising statements in that they give the child more detail into why this behavior is good for them now and in the future. For example, a statement that is more praising than affirming is "You did a great job studying for your tests, honey!" An affirming statement may sound like any of these:

→ "I noticed that you spent extra time studying for your test this week without the TV on and using your appropriate break times. Great job!"

→ "You really seem focused and have a plan for studying without distractions. I'm sure that will help you on the test."

→ "Studying like you just did will be a great skill for college!"

The extra details you add to affirming statements remind your child about the benefits of studying without distractions, plus it leads them to feel validated because you noticed their efforts.

In the beginning of any change in routine, it may be difficult to find opportunities to use affirming statements because the child may be struggling to adapt, but getting out the magnifying glass and finding the little morsels of effort being made will be worth your while.

Respect Their Autonomy and Competence

This part may be the most difficult, because it not only takes knowledge of what should be expected of your child at their age, but it also takes the willpower to allow the child to take some responsibility for their own progress.

As parents, we want to do all we can to support our child's performance, but for them to be able to succeed and grow their self-esteem, we must allow them to perform. It's important to remember that even though you can reflect and brainstorm with your child about why these ideas to motivate them did or didn't work, ultimately, you can't force them to change. And change in motivation or performance rarely happens overnight.

For self-esteem to grow, it's important for children to see themselves as competent and capable of change and growth. If there's something that they can do on their own and you do it for them, you're potentially robbing them of the opportunity to feel a sense of accomplishment. There are other ways you can help. If, for example, your child has great working memory and knows exactly what homework is due and when, but can't focus long enough to finish the homework, allow her to be able to have control of remembering her work in a way that she sees fit, but then help her with focus and attention using the strategies in chapter 8 (see page 131). And if your child has shown they can do it, let them do it.

PART TWO

Building Your Child's Executive Function

It's time to get strategizing! The chapters in part 2 will give you concrete strategies to help develop and strengthen life skills that can boost your child's executive functioning. Each chapter will address a different area, including:

→ Practicing self-control

→ Regulating emotions

→ Boosting memory

→ Creating and following routines

→ Staying focused

→ Managing time wisely

→ Building resilience

Within each area of skill, we'll explore:

→ Habits that can help develop the particular skill

→ How to address specific problems that arise from that particular skill deficit

→ Ideas for supporting performance at school

You'll also find tips for avoiding common parenting mistakes when addressing the particular skill, fun game ideas to help work on the skill, and some personal "life hacks" from my own experience living with ADHD.

Practicing Self-Control

If you are a parent of a child with ADHD or executive functioning issues, you probably know about impulse control. You may remember the fear when you would stand at a crosswalk wondering if your child would dart into traffic because they dropped their toy. Controlling our impulses may be the single most important executive functioning skill to develop in order to become a happy and healthy adult. In this chapter, we'll discuss ways for you to help your child control their impulses, some typical struggles that come along with a child's lack of impulse control, and different ways to parent a child who exhibits a lack of self-control.

Set Them Up for Success

The good news is we've learned a lot about how we can help a child develop better self-control. Use the strategies in this section to build simple habits that can improve your child's self-control.

Hit the Pause Button

If your child struggles with impulse control, their brain is basically working too fast, and they need an opportunity to slow it down. In these moments, you can simply say, "I want you to stop for 30 seconds and think about that decision."

You can use this technique for impulsive kids of all ages. Before you implement this strategy, though, you'll want to sit down with them and have a discussion letting them know what the word "pause" means. This way, you can just say the word "pause" and give them the chance to slow that brain down a bit to think through all the potential effects of their decision. For younger kids, you could choose a funny word or hand signal together that gives them the opportunity to pause and think through potential outcomes.

Catch Moments of Control

Even if your child seems like the most impulsive kid in the world, they still will have moments of calm when they are more in control of themselves. It's important to catch these times and help them see that they are practicing self-control, because it affirms their effort and helps them know they can do it. It's also a good reminder to you that they are, indeed, capable of controlling their impulses.

You can also do a little detective work to see what helps their self-control. In this moment, can you notice if the situation, time of day, or internal self-talk of the child led to their ability to control their actions? This information can be useful to use in the future when helping them reflect on their impulse control or lack thereof.

For example, if you catch your impulsive child blurting out a word interrupting you, but they then quickly close their mouth to stop themselves, you can immediately ask them, "How did you do that?" You want to encourage their effort to control themselves from interrupting you; you also want to understand what in that split second stopped them from continuing to interrupt you. If they respond, "I don't know," you can throw out some possibilities, like:

→ "Were you thinking about what might happen if you kept talking?"
→ "Were you thinking about how I would have felt if you kept interrupting me?"
→ "Did you remember interrupting your sister after school the other day?"

These types of questions can help imprint positive ways to control themselves on their brain so they remember in the future. It may be difficult for you to do as a parent, so try to be mindful daily about finding these successes. You can remind yourself by setting a reminder on your phone or to-do list, or by keeping a nightly journal.

Foster Awareness

The first step toward any change is awareness. We need to know there is a problem before we can solve it. So when it comes to a child's impulsive behaviors, we need them to gain an awareness of typical impulsive behaviors, what they are thinking when they make impulsive decisions, when are some times that they act the most impulsively, and ways to stop themselves when they act impulsively. This awareness can be fostered in many ways.

For kids about 8 years old and up, you can start a daily journal with your child and go over when they made an impulsive decision, what they were thinking, and what they could do differently if they were able to slow their brain down. It is not meant to be a punishment, but rather a way to sit together and reflect so they can build that prefrontal cortex part of the brain. You can also discuss and help them understand their physical cues when they act impulsively. Do they feel a burst of energy throughout their body? Does their breathing get more rapid? Or do they feel nothing? No matter what the reason, helping your child start to recognize and understand their body's cues can help them better understand their impulsivity.

Another strategy to help with impulsivity is teaching mindfulness to your children. Studies have shown that increased practice of meditation and mindfulness can decrease impulsive behaviors. Mindfulness is basically slowing your thoughts down to only think about the present moment. Children with ADHD and executive functioning weaknesses do not do this naturally. Their thoughts seemingly dart around like a hummingbird looking for a flower!

Meditation and mindfulness can help them practice slowing down their brain to be more aware of themselves and the moment, and hopefully gives them the time and bandwidth to make the right decision. You can download a number of different apps on your phone or use YouTube to look up programs that would work for you and your child in this area. See some suggestions in the Resources section (page 181).

Handling Impulsive Behaviors

When a child has difficulty practicing self-control, they will often engage in some maladaptive behaviors. They may lie, grab toys from friends, or sneak food to keep in their room— and older kids may engage in riskier behaviors. With these problem behaviors come some unique challenges for parents. Here we will go over a few of these challenges, and pitfalls to avoid when addressing them.

Lying

Children with ADHD seem to lie more than children without ADHD. Sometimes it is a learned behavior that they've seen work to help get them what they want, but oftentimes for children with ADHD it's simply an inability to practice self-control. As an adult with ADHD, I'll admit that sometimes little white lies come out of me for no real reason. If my wife asks me how long it took to mow the lawn, I may say 45 minutes rather than 30. I don't gain much from saying it was 45 minutes instead of 30 minutes, other than the fact that I look like I worked 15 extra minutes. I've learned to either catch myself immediately after or come back and say, "I don't know why I said that, but it was actually 30 minutes." Ultimately, that is what we want for our kids. If they impulsively lie and we know it, we can give them a few seconds to think about it, which helps them slow their brain down, but it also helps you know whether they're really lying to manipulate or if it was just an impulsive reaction. If you give them a few minutes to think about their lie and they stick with it, then you know it's not just an impulsive slipup.

If you can catch your child in what you know is a lie, don't panic. Lying does not mean that your child is a bad person or that you did a bad job as a parent. It could just be an inability to control their impulses. By telling yourself this, hopefully you can maintain that authoritative parenting style we discussed in chapter 2 (see page 25). Maintaining calm and approaching the lie in a reasonable and matter-of-fact way is the first step to addressing a lie with your child.

The next step would be to give them that pause button that we discussed earlier. Give them 30 seconds to think things through. If they stick with the lie, again, don't panic. In my practice, I've noted that many great kids with ADHD and executive functioning skills lie—and stick with the lie.

For kids 8 and older, a next step would be to calmly mention the evidence you have. Treat it almost like a mini-courtroom. If your child is lying by saying they turned in their homework, you can calmly mention that you saw online that they have a zero for the assignment and the teacher is good about posting grades daily and on time.

If they continue to stick to their story, give them a chance to provide evidence. If they cannot provide evidence, then you may think about what can motivate them; in this case, to get the homework done. Be sure to do this without mentioning lying. Just mention the evidence. This may sound like, "Once I have evidence that you've done this homework, then you can play your video games."

By doing this, you are not accusing or placing blame. You are just providing the facts and your expectations. Children with ADHD or executive functioning issues already feel blamed too often, so it's a healthy approach to express what you need in a way that doesn't add to these feelings.

Defiance

Almost 40 percent of children with ADHD develop oppositional defiance disorder (ODD), a condition marked by severe angry outbursts, annoying behavior, and a strong tendency to argue. Oftentimes they display defiant behavior just from an impulsive default.

Although your child with ADHD and executive functioning disorder may not be diagnosed with ODD, they may still display defiant behavior. They may stomp their foot and say, "NO!" to your request to pick up their toys. They may impulsively say, "I'm not going to do that," when you ask them to take out the trash. Teenagers may sneak out of the house when they know that they should not. This defiance is at least somewhat related to a lack of impulse control. The child is acting on what is most desirable to them in the moment. They aren't thinking about why you're asking them to do something that they don't want, or how saying no in the moment affects the whole family.

With children between ages 4 and 7, you can help them plot out their course of action with words. For example, if your child says no to picking up their toys, you can give them choices of what may happen if they stick to their defiant guns—because they are so "in the moment," they may not be processing their choices at all. You might say, "If you choose to not pick up your toys, you may have to go to bed early. If you choose to pick up your toys now, you will get to have your story time like usual." It's important to keep consequences simple and avoid rewarding the child just to do their expected job. If we say, "If you choose to pick up your toys now, you'll get extra story time," this becomes more like bribery, and can create more defiant behavior.

Children between ages 8 and 12 are usually ready to learn problem-solving skills in the moment. Oftentimes defiant behaviors come from not knowing in that moment how to solve a problem or meet their needs. If your child says that they will not take the trash out later, your first instinct may be to assure them that they will definitely be doing so, or else. But that kind of power struggle with a child with ADHD or executive functioning deficits can end up in an explosion.

To avoid that, you can say (in that same authoritative way), "So the problem is that I want you to take out the trash after dinner and you don't want to do that. How can we solve this in a way that works for both of us?" Hopefully, they will then offer some solution that they themselves can come up with, and you can respond whether that solution is doable or not.

If they say that they just don't want to do it, you can explain why you want them to do this job. "I need you to take the garbage out before tomorrow morning because that's when the trash pickup is. We don't want to have smelly trash in our house." If you explain why you want them to take out the trash, you're giving them an opportunity for their brain to slow down and think about your request and the maintenance of the household. Hopefully, this will lead them to get off the video game and take out the trash. If it doesn't, you can then mention the potential consequences, but at least you have helped them think things through.

Over-Apologizing

Children with impulse control issues often make a lot of mistakes. They need a lot of redirection. Many feel a significant amount of guilt. Over time, they may develop a pattern of expecting that they are making mistakes, and apologizing for perceived mistakes that aren't really mistakes.

This is something I see with many children that I work with in junior high and early high school—in fact, I felt this way myself. I thought that I was constantly making mistakes and needed to make up for all of them. I apologized to friends, teachers, and others even before I made mistakes. It became annoying and difficult for others around me. I would apologize for just about anything. If I played ping-pong and won a shot but the other person had to walk a few feet to get the ball, I apologized. If I asked a friend a question, I would start it off with an apology.

If you have a child who impulsively over-apologizes, try to catch them when they apologize. First, recognize that they are already feeling some level of guilt, so there's no need to criticize them for over-apologizing. Second, help them ask themselves two questions:

→ Did I intend to hurt someone or was I careless?
→ Did I do something that was completely unexpected in the situation?

If the answer is "no" to both questions, tell them they don't have to apologize. After practicing this approach, the next time you catch them over-apologizing, simply say, "Ask yourself the two questions." Saying this will remind them to pause and think about whether they really need to apologize. Once I stopped over-apologizing and began to apologize only for appropriate mistakes, my thoughts became less focused on what I was doing wrong and more about taking appropriate responsibility when needed. This approach also led to more confidence and less anxiety.

School Support

As much as you can support your child at home, they are at school for much of their day. Therefore, it's important to help support an environment that addresses your child's unique executive functioning strengths and weaknesses.

In my counseling practice, I often attend school meetings to help create individualized education plans for students. These plans are designed to help address impulse control issues as well as other issues. I have found that most teachers really want to help children and are open to trying new ways to support children with unique executive functioning needs. There are many different techniques that teachers use to help children learn to practice self-control in classrooms.

STOP AND THINK SIGNALS – Many teachers will help children between the ages of 4 and 7 by providing them with "Stop and Think" cards that they place on the child's desk when they notice them engaging in impulsive behavior. This concept can be adapted to include a secret signal, like placing a red card on the dry erase board that gives the child a signal. Any kind of visual will do, but the child must first buy into the idea, so it's best to have a discussion with the child regarding what kind of signal they are comfortable with. If they don't buy into this strategy, it may become something that they avoid or are ashamed of, so we want to give them some control and choice in the development of these signals and plans.

GENTLE REDIRECTION – A common tactic used by teachers is to give the student consistent and brief reminders to manage their impulsivity. This tactic simply involves the teacher paying a little bit more attention to the child to make sure that they are controlling their impulses. It is best done in a subtle, nonjudgmental way, with as few words as possible, to make sure that the child doesn't feel ashamed or lose focus. For example, if an 8-year-old boy with impulse control issues is touching his neighbor constantly, the teacher may just say, "James. Hands." This short instruction leads to less confusion and embarrassment in the child that often has all eyes on him. Simple redirections like this can preserve the child's self-esteem.

I always suggest that, when asking teachers to use any simple tips like these, parents try to pour on the empathy and then give a simple explanation. This may sound like, "I know it's tough with so many children in the classroom. And I don't expect perfection from my child or you. I just think that a few subtle words would help him redirect without getting embarrassed and potentially shutting down." Teachers have a tough job and appreciate knowing that you are on the same team, so it can really make a difference to give them that empathy when asking for accommodations.

What to Avoid

We know that parenting a child who struggles with self-control can be exhausting and frustrating. Oftentimes we parents use labels or all-or-nothing statements when we're frustrated. We may say, "You always make the same mistake over and over again," or "How can you be so thoughtless?" These statements are damaging because they label the child as a careless and thoughtless person, rather than a child who had a careless or thoughtless moment.

For parents, it's important to de-personalize the complaint. Instead of "Why are you always interrupting?" you might explain, "When you interrupt your grandparents, it can be frustrating to them." This way, you are labeling the impulsive behavior rather than judging them as a person, because as we know, they are more than just an impulsive person—they are a funny, smart, and inspirational kid who isn't defined by their impulsivity.

Many parents of impulsive children tend to be impulsive themselves. As such, it becomes an extra challenge to manage our own impulsive reactions to the child's impulsivity. If you do react in an impulsive fashion, it's completely okay to come back and apologize to your child for saying something that you regret. It will feel good, and it's great to model that behavior for them. You're saying, *We **all** make mistakes!*

An authoritarian parent will probably never admit their mistakes, because as they see it, they are the ones in control and anything they say is right, yet they can be firm but also apologetic when they're wrong. This may sound like, "I am sorry. I was really frustrated and said that you always make the same mistakes. There are times when you are able to manage your impulses. I recognize that. But I need you to know that when you sneak food from the kitchen at night when you know you're not supposed to, there will be a consequence." No matter what kind of parenting style you possess, there is a way to make things right.

Make It Fun!

There are a lot of fun ways to practice self-control; in fact, the ability to control impulses is the basis for many common games. With younger children, you can play classics like Simon Says, Red Light/Green Light, Freeze Tag, or Duck, Duck, Goose. All these games require children to stay still or act upon directions from another person.

For older children 8 years and up, you can play a game called Pick 'Em Up. All you need are different objects in different colors and a few players. Set out a variety of items. These items could be five black pens, five pieces of white paper, and four red balls. You'll have three rounds of increasing difficulty with the two teams of players.

In the first round, you'll replace the names of the colors with something else. You may say that the color black is now named white, the color white is now named red, and the color red is now named black. (You can write these changes on a piece of paper to remember them.) Then you say, "The first team to pick up three red things and two white things wins this round—and, go!" The players now have to inhibit their impulse to pick up three red balls and two pieces of white paper, and instead pick up three sheets of white paper and two black pens instead. To increase the difficulty, change the names of the items along with the colors.

Another simple and quick way to practice self-control around the dinner table is The Question Game. This is a game for the family in which you pick a topic and then must go around in a circle and ask each other questions about that topic. The trick is that you cannot answer the question, and you must immediately respond with a question that is on topic. The first person to respond with an answer or who cannot respond in time is out. Continue to play until there is just one person left.

For example, you all agree that the topic will be movies. The mother starts by asking the daughter, "Did you ever see *Frozen?*" The daughter then says, "Of course!" The daughter is then "out" for that round, as she didn't respond with a question. The son responds with "Do you like Marvel movies?" The father resists the impulse to answer, and instead asks the mother, "Have you ever seen a movie over four hours long?" They keep going until one of them responds with a statement and not a question. To increase the difficulty, you can say that the players only have two seconds to respond.

Pro Tip

Reining in my impulses took most of my childhood and even a lot of my 20s to be able to master. Okay, admittedly I have not mastered it yet, but I've gotten a little bit better over the years. My current impulsive behavior that gets me in the most trouble is eating something sweet at night. If it's there, I have to have it! But I've learned over the years that my survival in life doesn't depend on Blue Bell ice cream.

Much of our impulsive behavior comes from the misguided assumption that we need something when we really just *want* it or *would like to have* it. For children with ADHD or executive functioning issues, the need can feel very real!

Talk to your child about the difference between needs and wants. You can even have your child come up with a list of their needs and wants and rank them in importance, or give them a number of 1 out of 10. This way they can see more concretely that their wants may feel important to them in the moment, but they're not really a necessity. You can even post this list somewhere as a reminder about what's most important and what they don't have to have right this moment.

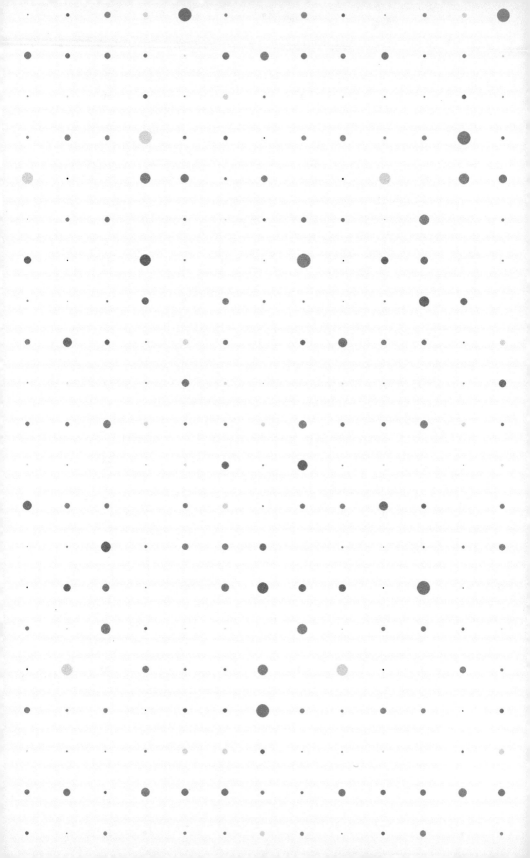

Regulating Emotions

Between ages 2 and 6, a child starts to develop emotional regulation, or the ability to manage feelings, which is an essential skill for the development of relationships, academic performance, and resilience. To successfully manage their feelings, children must be able to remember and learn from past experiences and make connections between their behaviors and consequences. They must be able to think of multiple solutions to a problem. And they must be able to catch themselves from reacting impulsively due to their emotional state. As you can see, emotional regulation makes use of many different executive functioning skills. In this chapter, you'll learn age-appropriate ways to help build emotional regulation in your child.

Set Them Up for Success

If your 5-year-old yells every time you ask them to do something mildly uncomfortable, or if your 9-year-old slams a game controller every time they are eliminated in a video game, or your 12-year-old regularly throws things in anger, they are lacking emotional regulation skills. This is not the time to punish the behavior, but rather to teach them more productive ways to express their emotions so they're better equipped to deal with life's stumbling blocks in the future.

Stay Calm

It can be tough to deal with a child who is acting out without losing your own cool. Children are great observers of how we are feeling, but often misperceive what we are feeling. They often think that their parent is much angrier with them than they are. This misperception can lead to anxiety if they think that their parents are consistently frustrated, angry, or disappointed in them. Before you can effectively address your child's emotional outburst, you'll want to regulate your emotions so you can be the calm in the storm.

According to the authors of the book *When Anger Hurts Your Kids*, children of parents who have problems regulating their own anger are often more noncompliant and aggressive, less empathetic, and grow to have overall poor adjustment in adulthood. Indeed, parental anger can continue to impact children into adulthood, increasing the likelihood of depression, social alienation, and spousal abuse, as well as impaired career and economic achievement.

As we work toward being that calm in the storm, we must pinpoint what beliefs are causing us to be angry in that moment. Here are some assumptions that might lead a parent to overreact:

→ "Children should always listen to their parents."
→ "If this child is behaving this way at 5 years old, they're going to be so much worse at 12 years old."
→ "If this child is acting like this, other people will think I'm an awful parent, so I have to get them to stop whatever way I can."
→ "I do so much for this child, and they are disrespecting me. That is not fair to me!"
→ "This behavior will never get better!"

If you hold any of these beliefs, ask yourself whether it is actually true. List evidence to challenge some of these assumptions. Some of these beliefs are more harmful than helpful and can lead to more frustration.

You don't need to hide or minimize your feelings—it's more about making sure that your child knows that you're responsible for your feelings, just like they are responsible for theirs.

If you need to take a break to calm down, that's okay. Allow yourself to walk away for a moment as long as the child is safe and not hurting themselves or others. Once you feel centered, come back and address your child's behavior. Go ahead and apologize to them if you let your emotions get the best of you—this is a great way to normalize strong emotions and model appropriate ways to react to them.

Teach Emotional Awareness

Once you have successfully managed to stay calm, you can start to address your child's emotional regulation skill. Many children who are entering preschool and kindergarten aren't adept at calmly explaining their emotions like, "Mom, when you tell me to pick up my toys, I feel frustrated because I believe that you are not allowing me to have fun, and you know how important playtime is to me, right?" They aren't going to give an insightful and well-thought-out explanation for how they feel. The more likely default response probably involves yelling and throwing their toys. So you may need to help them develop emotional awareness.

WHERE DO YOU FEEL IT?

In moments of conflict, your goal as parents is to help the child become aware of their experience. Help them understand the sensations that they are feeling in their body, so they can connect that physical sensation with emotional language. If a child can learn to use their words, they are much less likely to use their fists. Calmly ask them where in their body they are feeling angry and to describe the feeling with words. You can even follow up later on by having them draw a picture of themselves and coloring in the part of the body where they felt that emotion.

REFLECTIVE LANGUAGE

Once you get your child to identify their emotions in the moment or after an outburst, help them summarize their experience using calm, reflective language. For example, you might say, "I hear that you are frustrated that you have to stop playing and clean up right now. You feel that frustration in your stomach and your fists." You may then want to offer up some alternatives to help them get unstuck from their negative thinking: "We'll read books in a few minutes. You can play with your toys again in the morning." Saying this shifts their focus away from a frustrating thought to a more desirable one, like knowing what they will get to do in the future or remembering that being uncomfortable doesn't last forever.

NONVERBAL CUES

For children ages 7 and up, you can help them become aware of their feelings in a more subtle way. For example, try giving them a "raised eyebrows" look, rather than immediately jumping in to say something. This is a less invasive cue you can use to help kids catch themselves in moments of emotional dysregulation. If that does not get them to pause, you may need to add in a question like, "What do you think I'm thinking right now?" or "Tell me what's going on," to help them pause and use language to solve the problem.

LABELING EMOTIONS

We want to help our children learn to process emotions verbally and understand them in a more effective way. Younger children around ages 4 and 5 may just state their feelings, like, "I feel angry," or "That makes me sad." For children ages 6 to 9, they hopefully can give some insight into why they feel a certain way, such as, "I feel angry because Corey called me a loser," or "I'm sad because I can't have an extra waffle this morning." Around age 10, many children can differentiate between their thoughts and their feelings. This may sound like, "I'm sad because when people make fun of me, it makes me think that I'll always be a loser," or "I'm angry because I feel like I don't get to make any decisions." Depending on their age, we want to help them along with verbalizing and understanding their feelings in an appropriate and helpful way.

AGES 4 TO 6: EMOTION WORD OF THE DAY

For children around 4 to 6 years old, a good goal is to begin adding to their emotional vocabulary. You can do this by having an emotion word of the day. Pick a card with an emotion word on it and try to use it five times that day in conversation.

You can also get a picture of different emojis displaying all kinds of emotions and display it somewhere prominent in the house. Kids can use it as a visual reference, pointing to how they feel, and then you can read the word out loud for them. This strategy may not work if a child is in the middle of a tantrum, for example, but you can use it after they've calmed down to reflect on their emotions and strengthen their emotional vocabulary for the future.

You can also focus on using reflective language in these years. This just means reflecting what they're feeling; for example, "You seem to be feeling frustrated that you don't get to have dessert before dinner." With the goal of expanding their emotional vocabulary, try to mix it up so your child can hear many different terms to describe a particular emotion.

AGES 7 AND 8: RATING EMOTIONS ON A SCALE

One goal for 7- and 8-year-olds is to enable them to understand their emotional spectrum so they can label their emotion and its intensity. Something I've done with many children is come up with an emotional rating scale using whatever their interest is. We label the scale from 1 to 5. Then we pick their currency to rate. They may use colors, superheroes, cars, Disney princesses—whatever they are interested in.

Using the scale, determine which of these items represents calmness to the child. For example, if the child has chosen colors, label the colors from 1 to 5, with larger numbers representing greater intensity. For example, green might represent calmness to a child, so it's labeled 1. The colors blue, yellow, orange, and red can follow, representing more intense levels of emotions. If they chose cars, the sedan can be 1 and the monster truck can be 5, with cars of graduating size and speed in between.

For the times that the child chooses an item between 2 and 5 in intensity, come up with two or three activities with your child that can help decrease the intensity of that undesired emotion, whether it's anger, anxiety, or sadness. I recommend that with greater intensity of the emotion, you use more physical activity involving big muscle groups, like riding a bike or jumping on a trampoline. For example, under "yellow," you may list "coloring" or "petting your dog," but for orange and red, you may have "jumping on a trampoline" or something more physically demanding.

AGES 9 AND UP: RECOGNIZING DISTORTED THINKING

Children who are 9 years old and older are starting to differentiate their thoughts from their feelings. They understand that just because they think something doesn't necessarily make it true. This kind of flexible thinking is more difficult for most children with ADHD and executive functioning weaknesses, but you can use simple and developmentally appropriate techniques to teach kids healthy ways to think about situations to manage emotions and behaviors.

One of the core concepts is identifying and reframing distorted thinking, which is an exaggerated or irrational thought pattern. As adults, if we are cut off in the road, our first instinct may be to honk to let others know that we shouldn't be messed with. But most adults are able to catch themselves and think, *I don't need to do that.* This thought reinterprets the situation, leading to better emotional and behavioral management.

To help tween-aged kids understand their distorted thinking and help them catch themselves and reframe it, use relatable examples. An example might be telling them a story about yourself, such as, "When I was a kid, I often thought that my teacher didn't like me because she never called on me. But then I thought, since I'm making good grades, maybe she didn't call on me because the other children need more help or confidence. That thought worked better for me." Give real and genuine examples, but nothing too heavy that will add anxiety to the child.

THOUGHT VILLAINS

The "Thought Villains" exercise uses superheroes that most kids are familiar with to explain common types of cognitive distortions. When addressing this issue, you can explain that these villains take over our brain and lead us to think thoughts that aren't true. They can also lead us to feel more intense feelings that we don't like. This knowledge motivates kids to want to identify and challenge them. Here's how you can describe the following Thought Villains to your adolescent, so they can identify when one comes on the scene.

APOCALYPSE – This villain is the biggest bad guy that there is. Apocalypse leads us to think of the worst-case scenario in a situation. For example, if you're on an airplane and experience some turbulence, you might automatically think, *The plane is crashing!* That is Apocalypse taking over your brain. To catch him, think of the more likely rational scenario to challenge him, such as the fact that flying is statistically the safest way to travel.

MR. ALL OR NOTHING – This villain may lead you to think that things are "always" bad or you "never" get what you want, which isn't exactly true. It exaggerates the way you think and leads to mistaken thinking that a little momentary discomfort will not change for the better. This may sound like, "I never get to play video games." Mr. All or Nothing usually leads to feelings of anger and helplessness, because he leaves no room for other possibilities or solutions.

MS. NEGATIVE – This villain will lead you to see only the negative in a situation, causing feelings of sadness and anger. Let's say you got your report card and it was the best one you've gotten in years, but you got an 89 in science when you wanted to make straight As. It's natural to be disappointed, but if you can't recognize how good your grades are overall because of the B, then maybe Ms. Negative is taking over your brain. It's okay to accept disappointment, but a more positive mindset allows you to try to see the whole picture.

PROFESSOR PERSONAL – He will lead you to think that it's your fault when something goes wrong, even when you're not to blame. He leads you to label yourself something bad that isn't true, causing you to feel guilty and sad. This may be thinking that since you struck out twice in a baseball game that it's ALL MY FAULT that you lost the game. In reality, you may not have played as well as you'd like, but it takes a whole team to lose or win. When Professor Personal takes over the brain, ask yourself to take the appropriate amount of responsibility—not too much.

Sit with your child and discuss these Thought Villains. Ask them which ones take over their brains most often. Can they relate to one or more of these villains? Share your own answers as well so your child can see that it's not just them— other people, even adults, have Thought Villains who try to take control of their thinking.

Depending on their age or interest level, you can have the child draw or find pictures online to represent each Thought Villain. Later, you can then catch your child thinking this way and say, "Which Thought Villain is taking over?" to get them to pause and catch themselves. When you discuss an incident where a child was unable to manage their emotions, you could use these visuals to help them understand if any of these villains impacted their thought process.

You know your child best. In the moment when a child is very upset, it may not be the best time to teach, so come back to this exercise when they are calmer. For children with ADHD, reflecting on what they are thinking with the Thought Villains may be difficult and tiring—short and simple often works best.

Solve the Problem

For many children with ADHD or executive functioning delays, their inability to communicate their needs efficiently or solve simple daily problems may be causing emotional outbursts. In his book *The Explosive Child*, Dr. Ross Greene explains that temper tantrums and challenging behaviors may actually just be the result of lagging skills. These children cannot get their needs met as effectively as other children, which leads to frustration. He recommends addressing these skill deficits using a collaborative three-step process of showing empathy, defining the problem, and inviting or brainstorming solutions. We'll explore this process here.

STEP 1: SHOW EMPATHY

The first step of the problem-solving model is intended to lower your child's guard and help you gather information about what is truly upsetting them. This step may feel counterintuitive, because when your 4-year-old is yelling because you poured his milk before getting his waffle, or your 10-year-old is slamming a game controller, your immediate reaction may be to try to reason with them or raise your voice. But this doesn't help either of you see the big picture.

Children with ADHD and executive functioning deficits tend to have thinking differences that are rarely communicated. I once worked with a 12-year-old who was diagnosed with ADHD. He would hit his brother, unprovoked, on a daily basis. Using the empathy step, I found out that he was trying to "toughen his brother up" to prepare him for bullies. He never verbalized this because he wasn't really even aware that was his motivation. He didn't have the communication skills to communicate his worry about his brother being bullied to his parents. He just acted on it. Once we figured out his real motivation, we were able to help him talk about his worries and support his brother in a more appropriate way.

Start with reflective listening as discussed in the "Labeling Emotions" section (page 83). Then say, "I've noticed that you have a problem when I ask you to get off the video game. What's up?" Saying this opens the door for more insight into their thought process. If they have trouble coming up with an answer, you can ask something like, "Tell me what thought led to you slamming the controller," or make an observation like, "I've noticed you only seem upset about this at night and not in the morning. What do you think is the reason for that?" Your goal in the empathy step is to understand more about their thought process and the real problem at hand, not just their behavior.

STEP 2: DEFINE THE PROBLEM

The second step is to clearly define the problem or state your concern. It's important to communicate this in a way that shows that you care for your child and that explains why developing this skill or practicing this behavior is good for them in the long run.

This may sound like, "I know that you feel angry and don't want to get off the game now, but you can't slam your game controller and yell. This behavior makes me feel worried. I don't want you to break your controller so you can't play anymore."

Children with ADHD and executive functioning weaknesses may need to hear how their behavior can lead to consequences that they don't like, but in a nonjudgmental way. The more they hear it in a nonjudgmental way, the more it will stick with them. By stating that you "feel worried" and you don't want them to break their controller so they can't play anymore, you are connecting how their behavior could potentially affect their future enjoyment of the game. When a child is frustrated, they often skip that step and don't think about the future or the consequences of their behavior, so they just simply act out their aggression.

STEP 3: INVITE SOLUTIONS

The final step in Dr. Greene's problem-solving model is to invite solutions. At this stage, you can brainstorm potential solutions that would be good for both you and your child. Make sure your child understands that the solutions are not about winning or getting everything they want (or everything we want), but something that is acceptable and doable for both sides.

This may sound like, "The problem is that you get really angry when you are asked to stop playing your video game at night, because you feel that this is the only time your friends are online and you can play. Playing with your friends is really important. What do you think we could do so you can play at night with your friends and not get so angry?"

If they don't come up with any ideas, you can suggest things that they can do differently, things that you could do differently, or things that they may tell themselves. For example, you may respond with, "I wonder if you got started on your homework 10 minutes earlier and we ate dinner 10 minutes later, whether you'd have enough time with your friends. That would be 20 extra minutes. Is that something you're okay with?"

It's important not to rush this step and force a solution on your child. Give them an opportunity to come up with their own solution, because independent problem-solving is the skill you are trying to develop in your child.

If you can't come to an agreement, you can say, "Let's take some time to think about it and talk tomorrow." Saying this may feel like giving in to what they want, but if you follow up an hour or a day later, you are giving them an opportunity to reflect and practice problem-solving on their own.

Boosting Emotional Regulation

When a child has difficulties with regulating emotions, they may show behaviors that are difficult to deal with as a parent. They may use aggression to solve their problems, react violently out of the blue, or express extreme sadness at unexpected times. In this section, we'll explore how to respond to these challenging behaviors and what to avoid when addressing them.

Mind Your Mind

One of the first things that I do when counseling a child who has difficulty regulating their emotions is to help them understand the simple brain science of what is going on when they are feeling strong emotions and acting out accordingly. By giving them a quick understanding of their brain, I can use some of the language to address these moments after the fact that is more accurate to their experience and does not involve shaming. I'll explain it to you so you can use it as well.

Dr. Dan Siegel, author of *The Whole-Brain Child*, uses a hand model to explain how the brain functions. To explain this model with children, try the following:

1. Open your hand out wide and then fold in your thumb. Explain that this thumb is the part of the brain that regulates their emotions.
2. Then fold four fingers over your thumb. Point to the middle two knuckles and say that this part of the brain is in control of making plans, thinking flexibly, and solving problems.
3. Slowly push out your thumb until your four fingers are standing up. Explain that the emotional part of your brain caused you to flip your lid. Explain that this leads to an alarm going off in the brain that is so loud that the thinking part of the brain doesn't work as well.
4. Brainstorm activities that can turn the alarm off, like taking deep breaths or squeezing something hard.

By understanding their brain and how it works in a simple and relatable way, you can turn to some of this language in the future, like "flipping your lid" or "sirens going off" rather than "you had a meltdown" or a "fit." This deeper awareness empowers them to help understand themselves and gives them hope to change.

Catch Success

Try your best to catch your child when they successfully manage their emotions, and give plenty of praise and encouragement. Studies show that an overly harsh parenting style and lack of praise can create even more issues with emotional regulation in a child, so it's pivotal for parents to focus on and celebrate positive behaviors whenever we can.

For children with executive functioning deficits, extra reminders in addition to encouragement will help them reflect on how they were able to manage their emotions. This means asking them to pause and explain how they were able to manage their emotions in that instance. For example, if your child was able to overcome their anxiety about jumping into the deep end of the pool, simply ask them, "How did you do that?" If they are typically frustrated and moody when you wake them up in the morning, but they're able to get up without the usual complaints, you may ask on the way to school, "You had a great morning! What did you tell yourself to not get angry like usual?" Saying this can help them reflect on their internal monologue and help you understand their inner workings a little better. This should work for children of all ages. Although older adolescents may roll their eyes, it's still worth the effort to see if you can get any moment of reflection from them.

Redirection

When your child is having trouble managing their emotions, try to engage them in activities that can help calm their body and their mind. For younger children, you may want to create a calming box with sensory toys, like putty, coloring books, balloons to blow up, or fidget toys.

Here are some other ideas for sensory breaks:

→ Create a chill-out corner they can turn to when they get stressed. Fill it with pillows or a beanbag chair, a weighted blanket, soft lighting, and/or a lava lamp.
→ Play a game of catch.

→ Put on their favorite music and let them dance.

→ Give them some putty or kinetic sand to play with.

→ Let them draw a face showing how they're feeling. Older kids can write how they're feeling without judgment. They can rip it up when they're done.

→ When your child is calm, have them write a reassuring note to their frustrated self. Hang the note so the child can see it when emotions rise.

→ Make a stress jar by filling a water bottle half with water, half with baby oil. Add some glitter, glue it shut, and let them turn it and watch the glitter drift around.

For children around ages 8 or 9, you may want to have a list of more physical activities that they can do. By calmly reminding them of these simple ways to redirect themselves rather than punishing or arguing, you're teaching them rather than expecting that they know how to manage their emotions. Over time, your child will know what works to calm themselves, and seek it out without prompting.

School Support

If your child is having trouble regulating their emotions at school, you can work with their teacher to give them some autonomy to take breaks. Suggest giving your child a simple break card in a color corresponding with an emotion. They can put the card on their desk to let the teacher know that they are feeling an emotion that needs to be addressed. It gives them the autonomy to take a break and go get a drink of water or visit a predetermined administrator that they have a positive rapport with, such as a school counselor.

Some elementary classrooms have a "cooldown" area with items like sensory toys, beanbag chairs, and a one-person trampoline that the child can use whenever they need to calm down. It gives the child some freedom to leave a stressful environment when they feel an intense feeling, because no one likes to have a breakdown in front of people.

What to Avoid

Children who have difficulty regulating their emotions and act impulsively can often back themselves into a corner. They may cross their arms, stomp their foot, and say, "I'm not budging!" This type of behavior is perplexing and frustrating to us as adults as we know that ultimately we have the power in the situation. It's important not to engage in the power struggle. Easier said than done, right?

The power struggle comes from your assumptions as a parent that the child's behavior in the moment means more than it does. It starts with what you tell yourself about the situation with your child. It's important to remember to stay in the moment and parent this moment in the appropriate way without reflecting on the past behavior or predicting future behavior.

You'll want to avoid threats of punishment when your child is having difficulty regulating their emotions—this only makes things worse. Their impulsivity doesn't allow them to fully process the consequences of their behaviors in that moment. They are just reacting on impulse in the moment, and engaging them with too many words can escalate the frustration. It doesn't mean that there should be no consequences or discussions if a child is outwardly defiant or violent, but it's best to first help them get to a place where they can calm down and reflect on their feelings and actions before you turn to consequences.

Make It Fun!

With younger children ages 4 to 6, you can have them draw a picture of their body and label where they feel each emotion in their body. They can use different colors to represent different emotions. Discuss how physical signs help us know when we are starting to feel a strong emotion. For example, you can draw red lines around the jaw to show that you clench your mouth when angry, or draw yellow squiggles in the stomach to represent "butterflies in the stomach" when anxious.

With children ages 9 and up, you can play a simple cognitive behavioral game called Thought Detectives. This game helps them understand how certain thoughts lead to strong emotions. Write or print a list of five thoughts. Here are some examples:

→ "Those two people are looking at me weird. They must be making fun of me."
→ "I'm never going to make the basketball team."
→ "This may be tough, but I think I can do it."

Then share a separate list of emotions. Ask the child to see how many emotions they can match with the different thoughts. If it won't overwhelm the child, you can set a timer to make it interesting. Then ask them to explain their answers one at a time. Ask them if they like the feeling that was listed, and if so, when can they use this thought in their life? If they don't like the feeling listed, they can brainstorm a different thought that can lead to more positive emotions.

There isn't a "right" answer in this game. The goal during this game isn't to tell a child how to feel, but rather to help them regulate feelings that they don't like or that lead them to do things they don't want to do.

Pro Tip

For younger children ages 4 and 5, always keep some simple fidgets or calming toys on hand, especially in the car, so you can offer them in the middle of a tantrum. You can also have an on-the-road playlist of calm music that your child likes.

For older children, have them practice a daily mantra that challenges some of their thoughts that lead them to feel intense feelings that they don't like. If they often get angry, because "Things are never fair!", you can invite them to say this mantra five times a day:

"I don't like it when things don't go my way. If I think things aren't fair, I can talk to my mom or dad and see if we can solve the problem. If we can't, that's okay because I can control my emotions."

This mantra is just a daily reminder to help them remember thoughts that could be helpful in managing their feelings.

For children ages 10 and up, use a cognitive behavioral app for in-the-moment help. Apps like CBT Thought Diary (see Resources, page 181) can help kids redirect and work through their thoughts and feelings. They can simply open the app and it will guide them through the process of reflecting on or challenging their thoughts. This app can work in the moment when the child feels distressed, or later, once they are calm.

Boosting Memory and Processing Speed

Our working memory is like a short-term storage system that allows us to store information needed to solve an immediate problem. The development of working memory is vital to a meaningful life and typically happens within the first three years of life. A working memory deficit is often first noticed when the child is age 8 or 9, as they begin being tasked with more complex directions in school and at home.

Children who struggle with working memory may have difficulty with reading and writing, repeat the same mistakes, and exhibit low self-esteem. Processing speed refers to the amount of time it takes for us to take in new information, make sense of it, and then respond using the new information that we have. Children with ADHD often display slower processing speed, which can lead to social and academic difficulties as well as the possibility of being labeled as less intelligent than they are. In this chapter, we'll explore tips for helping your child adapt their environment to help with their working memory deficits and to help them with forgetfulness.

Set Them Up for Success

Dr. Torkel Klingberg, a leading researcher on working memory, found that working memory is much like our muscles: flexible, moveable, and trainable. Working memory also affects the cognitive processing speed of children with ADHD. Although processing speed generally gets more efficient as a child grows, the gap between children with typical processing speed and slower processing speed doesn't close naturally. However, research suggests children with slower cognitive processing can grow in this area to process information more efficiently with the right interventions.

Get in Your Own Way

For children with ADHD or other executive functioning deficits, we need to look at the support we give to help their brain and working memory grow. But more important, we have to help them adapt their environment to account for their potential to forget information or lose important items. Here are some suggestions:

VISUAL CHORE LIST – For younger children, getting in their own way can look like putting a visual chore list in their play area.

DRY ERASE CALENDAR – For older adolescents, you may want to hang a big dry erase calendar right next to their gaming computer or on the door to their room. By having this calendar in an area that the child often views, they are learning how to get in their own way and adapt their environment to remind them of important things.

CALENDAR APPS/REMINDERS – Encourage older children to use calendar apps on their phone or smartphone reminders to keep track of important information. These children may need frequent reminders to use these apps, or the parents and children can set up the apps or alarms together on a weekly basis.

HOME BASE – For kids who may have difficulty remembering where things are, or are constantly rushing in the morning to find their bookbag or band instrument, it's important to have a home base in a high-traffic area where all important items go. I keep my keys and laptop and anything else that I need for work on the counter in our kitchen. This way, if I leave the bedroom or the living room, I must go past the kitchen counter to leave the house, so I will see it and remember to grab whatever is there before I leave. With younger kids, you can make it fun and create decorations for your home base.

By teaching a child to "get in their own way," you are helping them adapt their environment by giving themselves reminders.

Multisensory Learning

Physical activity has positive effects on our mood, but it also helps boost memory. In an interview with the *Harvard Health Letter*, neurology professor Dr. Scott McGinnis noted that engaging in a program of regular exercise at moderate intensity over six months to a year is associated with an increase in the volume of the brain region that controls memory. Who knew that we can grow our brain by exercising our body?

If your child has no interest in team sports, look for another way to integrate some sort of aerobic exercise into their week: jumping on a trampoline, jumping rope, skating, biking, swimming, or even just running around at a playground. The research shows that you do not need strenuous activity to improve your memory; just consistent aerobic exercise that gets your blood flowing will help grow the areas of the brain responsible for memory. You can see results in your memory by doing this exercise just three times a week for as little as 20 minutes! It can also reduce stress, which often inhibits the ability to hold multiple pieces of information in our working memory.

It may come as a surprise that moving while learning new information can be especially helpful for children with ADHD or executive functioning issues. Being active while learning new information increases the likelihood that information will transfer from the short-term memory part of our brain to the long-term memory part of our brain. There are many fun ways to do this, so get creative. For example, while practicing spelling, you can have your child bounce on an exercise ball, or play catch and throw a ball after every word they spell. Older children can simply walk around while they are trying to memorize something. You'll want to make sure that the movement or activity is not challenging or new to them, as that will distract from remembering the important information.

If you are a parent of a child with ADHD, you probably constantly need to remind your child with directions of things to do. If you have directions for your child, try to engage as many of their senses as possible to help them remember the information. For example, if you're in the kitchen, and you ask your child in the next room to take out the trash then set the table for dinner, you are relying on their hearing only to get information to their brain. But if you can walk to their room, touch them on the shoulder, look at them, and say, "It's time to take out the trash and get the table ready for dinner," you're using three different senses: hearing, touch, and sight.

This multisensory approach could also be used to help a child with ADHD study and retain information in both the short and long term. For example, non-distracting instrumental music may help during study sessions, or chewing on mints or gum can engage your child's sense of taste while reading or taking in new information.

Allow for More Time

Sometimes children with working memory delays or slower cognitive processing speed simply need more time to finish a task. They may also need more time to respond to simple instructions. It's not fair to expect that all children can just plow through work quickly, so if your child seems to process information a little more slowly than their siblings, it's okay to give them extra time to finish their work and adjust expectations about the time that a task may take for them to complete.

It's important for parents to stay patient with the child and give them extra breaks when engaging in any work, whether it's studying or doing chores around the house. These children tend to wilt under the pressure of a ticking clock, so try to avoid giving them time limits when you give them a task. If you are rushing out the door and ask them to grab their backpack, turn off the lights, and feed the dog all within a short amount of time, you may be setting your child up for failure. If you want your child to complete those tasks before leaving the house, this might mean waking up a little earlier to provide your child with enough time to complete everything that they need to do.

You may also need to check in with them. This may sound like, "I see that you've got your backpack and the lights are off in your room. What do you think you need to do next?" It may be more time-consuming for you, but you're helping them by planning ahead and making the tasks more manageable for them.

Handling Forgetfulness

Children with ADHD or other executive functioning issues are capable of remembering and retrieving information—it just takes them longer to do it. Here are a few activities and tricks you can use to help your child learn how to retrieve information.

Play Detective

You may remember the old TV show *Columbo* from the '70 (or maybe not!) that features a detective who always pretended not to know and basically tricked criminals into telling the truth. In therapy, this method of questioning is a common technique to get to the truth or to get the most relevant information from a client. You can use this technique to boost your child's memory, because it teaches them how to retrieve information and how to ask themselves questions to recall information that they forget.

Let's say your 12-year-old knows that they brought their science book home, but they can't find it. Instead of jumping in with the typical idea of retracing their steps, ask some open-ended questions to help jog their memory. Doing so will teach them how they can jog their own memory in the future. For example, you might ask:

→ "Where do you most often have your book?"
→ "When is the last time you opened your backpack, and where were you? Do you remember hearing anything or feeling anything?"
→ "I wonder how we could remember where this book is in the future."

The beauty of this technique is that it helps jog their memory in a very nonjudgmental way. I know I feel more anxious and am less likely to remember something important if someone is reminding me about the mistakes I made in the past, how I keep repeating them, or what I should have done instead—and the same logic holds true for kids.

Chunking Technique

Another way to help your child learn to recall information more efficiently is to use the "chunking" technique. Have you ever picked up your child from school and asked them what they learned, only for them to grunt, "Nothing"? This response may be their way of avoiding the question, but it also could be that nothing comes to mind quickly. By grouping or "chunking" information, we can help them retrieve information more effectively.

Instead of asking what happened today in general, try being more specific. For example, you might say, "Tell me three things you noticed about science class." The three things might include that they noticed that the teacher's perfume was really strong or that their friend got in trouble for talking. Then you can follow up with asking about something they learned, in which case they may make a connection between the lesson and the perfume they smelled or when their friend got in trouble. The hope is that they'll learn to make connections from what they do remember to help them with what they may have forgotten.

With younger children around ages 5 to 7, you may just want to model your own process for remembering information verbally. If you forgot something and are looking for it, simply verbalize your thought process so they can follow along. For example, let's say you are looking for your keys and you ask your child to help. You may say, "I normally leave my keys on the counter, but they're not there. Where are other places I've left my keys recently? Hmm, I know that I wouldn't ever take them to the bathroom (insert chuckle here). Could anyone else have taken them? Oh, yeah, your dad needed the keys to move the car yesterday; he probably left them by the bed. Here they are!" By narrating your thought process, you are modeling positive self-talk and problem-solving to help your child know how to handle their own forgetfulness in the future.

Ask Leading Questions

Slow processing speed and lagging working memory make it difficult to get started on tasks, especially when they require multiple steps. Even if a task itself only takes two steps, sometimes children can forget where to start. It can lead to frustration with the parent, who may think the child is being defiant. Assuming negative intent in this way makes it impossible to relate to their child's struggle to initiate, since the parent can likely do it without thinking about it.

It is a good idea to give your child with memory struggles and slower processing speed a little more time to start a task. If you ask your 3rd grader with working memory deficits to start their homework, they may feel lost. Instead, try asking them, "Do you have any questions about how to start?" or "What do you think is the best way to start your homework or the first step to finishing your homework?" These questions help them learn to initiate tasks for themselves. If your child is younger than 7 years old, you may find it helpful to give them one visual reminder when each step is finished, rather than multi-step directions.

We also need to be there to patiently guide them while they are working through the problem. You might ask your child, "What do you need from me to get your homework started?" By making yourself available, you are planting the seeds for them to advocate for themselves and ask for help. Children with memory issues or slower processing speed who can advocate for themselves will feel more empowered and confident in the long run.

Write It Down

Many children with ADHD or executive functioning issues tend to be visual learners rather than auditory, learning better with visual cues and experiencing things hands-on rather than by following verbal instructions. The problem with retrieving information is that it often requires thinking about words without seeing the information.

To help younger children around ages 5 to 7, ask them to draw a quick picture of some important information they may need to recall and put it somewhere where they know they will see it. For 8- to 12-year-olds, you may ask them to write down as much information about something they are trying to recall as possible. You can have a small dry erase board called a "memory board," where your child can doodle or write down key phrases to help them recall information visually in an attempt to help jog their memory.

To illustrate this idea, let's say your 10-year-old son can't find the gift he was going to give his sister for her birthday that he stashed away a month ago. He can get the dry erase board and write down words that are associated with buying and storing the gift, and where he would or wouldn't hide it. He may write "toy store," "not in the closet," "not in mom and dad's room," "I bought it last month on a weekend," or "I remember coming home and swimming." Although this activity may or may not help your child remember the information they need, you're teaching an important process of retracing steps that they can use on their own.

School Support

A typical school environment often addresses self-control, emotional regulation, and lack of focus and attention with accommodations for children with ADHD or other executive functioning issues, but it rarely addresses issues with slow processing speed and working memory. This gap in support can lead these children to feel like failures in school and avoid competitive environments altogether. If teachers know to accommodate these children in a few simple ways, they can make a world of difference for the child with processing speed or memory issues.

Remove Time Pressure

Children with slower processing skills are at a disadvantage, especially with timed tests or when class participation depends on how quickly they can raise their hand. One way to address this is for teachers to avoid timed tests or quizzes for children with slow processing speed or memory issues. They can offer a "buffer time" when quizzing the class or asking questions students are expected to answer, meaning that they can give a 10-second buffer before picking a child to answer the question. This strategy is a great way to reinforce self-control, equal opportunity for all students, and the merits of getting the right answer instead of being the first student to answer a question.

Show the Final Product

To help children with working memory issues follow multi-step directions, teachers can show a completed version of a long-term project. Doing so gives the child a visual reference to go back to and remind themselves what step comes next. For example, if a teacher wants to assign a class presentation on a historical figure, they can show an example of a previous student's project, complete with pictures and a guide listing what they did and how they completed the assignment. This gives the child something concrete to go back to so they don't get lost in the multi-step process, and the visual aids can help them remember the process for future projects.

Provide Notes to Fill In

Children with working memory issues and slower processing speeds often struggle with handwriting and note-taking. They are so focused on the writing part of note-taking that there is little retention of the actual information.

To get around this issue, teachers can give students a copy of notes that they need to take with some blanks to fill in. Doing so forces the child to pay enough attention to retain key information, but eases the burden of having to write everything down. This strategy can help kids remember more content from lectures, and as a result, they will be more prepared and hopefully need less review time before tests.

What to Avoid

As mentioned before, it is important not to overwhelm a child who struggles with memory or processing speed with too many instructions at once. It not only sets the child up for failure, but will also set you up for unnecessary frustration.

Children with memory issues can shut down if given too much verbal information. The worst thing anyone can do in response to these issues is to give a long-winded lecture about forgetfulness! The most helpful way to address this issue is to keep instructions and redirections as short and simple as possible in a supportive manner.

It is also important not to demand quick responses or transitions from one activity to another. If children are continually demanded to do something they simply cannot do because of their memory issues, it can lead to low self-esteem and frustration with simple requests. More effective approaches include warnings of transitions or requirements and enough time to think and respond.

Make It Fun!

There are tons of online games or programs out there that promise to help develop your memory. This promise can be misleading, as many studies have shown that they may only help with specific tasks like the ones being tested in the game.

However, we can take popular games and use them to help the child reflect on how they were able to use their memory in the game. For example, you can play the popular matching game in which players take turns flipping over a pair of cards and try to remember the cards with matching patterns. After every successful match, you can ask them to explain how they remembered that match. The act of verbalizing their retrieval process can help them with that process in the future.

You can also play the "I went shopping" game. To play, everyone takes a turn saying, "I went shopping and I bought a . . ." For each turn, a player adds an item to the list. The winner is the last person who can remember all the items correctly.

In addition to playing the game, you'll want to prompt kids to reflect and ask how they remembered the items, so you both learn what works best for them—whether it's visually thinking of pictures of the items, mnemonically remembering the items, or just connecting the item with the person who said it. You'll then know which strategies to encourage in the future.

Pro Tip

If your child doesn't have their phone or notebook with them to jot down information they will need to remember, encourage them to "sit" with the information. This simply means to prompt them to visualize when they will need that information in the future. This simple visualization technique helps your child by giving them a preemptive reminder of what they are expected to do or remember. By creating a picture in their head of when they will need the information, they are given a point of reference.

Let's say that you're taking your child from school back home for a quick snack and then to soccer practice. If your child says that she remembers that her cleats are outside rather than in her room like usual, you can ask her to take 10 seconds to visualize walking through the door, going to the backyard, and getting her cleats, and then going to her room to get changed. This visualization gives her a reminder about some important information that she may otherwise forget. This way, if she walks inside and forgets that her cleats are outside, she can just replay the visual script and then recall the information she needs.

CHAPTER
SEVEN

Creating and Following Routines

Children as young as age 2 can start to benefit from having a daily routine. Daily and weekly routines help ease anxiety in children by providing predictability and security. The stability of a predictable environment can also help develop memory and reduce impulsive behaviors. In this chapter, we'll visit strategies for establishing simple but effective routines for your child. You'll also get tips for teaching them to create routines for themselves.

Set Them Up for Success

Researcher Dr. Phillippa Lally and other researchers at University College London determined that we must do an activity for 66 days in a row before it becomes a habit. And this finding comes from research for adults who do not have a diagnosis of ADHD. The same research noted that the ability to develop and follow routines is a skill that can lead to increased productivity and greater satisfaction with life in adulthood. Here are some general strategies you can use to help kids practice creating a routine that works for them.

Get Their Buy-In

A child who is involved in the process of creating and developing family routines is more likely to follow through on them. If you create a daily routine without engaging your kids, you are losing out on the opportunity to help them develop the skill of negotiating and prioritizing their time.

For 4- to 7-year-olds, this may look like a simple discussion focused around three key points:

1. What is a routine and why do we have them?
2. What are two or three things you want to get out of your day (for example, see a friend, go to the park, bake something, paint their nails, play video games)?
3. How can you best remember the routine? (For a younger child, suggestions might include posting reminders in locations they choose.)

This discussion should take only a few minutes. If it's difficult for them to focus on the discussion, create a visual to grab their attention. You can show a step-by-step chart with pictures showing what's expected of them. For example, show a picture of a family having dinner, with a clock showing the time if they can tell time. Then follow that with a picture of a bathtub or whatever you need your kid to do. Next, ask them what they want from their day and how they can fit it into the schedule.

Remember that your main goal is to learn about your child's priorities and help them practice organizing their time. If they insist on staying up all night, then you may simply ask, "What would you do all night with your time?" Asking this can give you insight into what they may want to integrate into their day, so you can help them prioritize and plan for it.

For children ages 8 to 12, who can attend a family meeting for up to five minutes at a time, you may want to focus on some similar points in a discussion that are slightly different, like:

→ How is this routine important to your life now and in your future as an adult?
→ What are one or two things you want from your day?
→ How can you best remember this routine, and do you need a visual reminder or list?
→ What are some things that may get in the way of creating or following this routine?

The last question helps kids problem-solve and learn to develop routines that work for them and their potential executive functioning strengths and weaknesses. We don't ask this of younger children because it takes a level of self-awareness they may not yet possess.

Your child may respond that they might have trouble remembering the routines, or that when they are in a bad mood they won't want to follow them. Once you have this information, you can help them find ways to address potential pitfalls and help them create routines to get around them. It may involve giving them more visual reminders of routines if they are forgetful, or allowing a little downtime if they are generally tired immediately after school.

Understanding your child's concerns and getting them to buy into the plan helps them develop routines that work for them, and it can also help you create daily routines that stick, smoothing the path for a successful day.

Connect Routines to Goals

One of the common concerns that I hear from parents is that their teenagers with ADHD lack direction and don't follow through with daily routines. A child's apparent lack of motivation may stem from underdeveloped executive functioning skills. Due to memory, impulsivity, and attention difficulties, children with ADHD and other executive functioning weaknesses need help connecting their present routines to future outcomes—even as teens.

Adolescents with ADHD can benefit from a goal-driven daily or weekly routine. This routine is especially helpful for a child who is developing a new skill or trying to improve at something they are passionate about. To illustrate how you can create routines based on goals that are personally meaningful to your child, let's use the example of my client, a 12-year-old with ADHD, whom we'll call Gavin.

Gavin is passionate about baseball. His father was frustrated because he saw Gavin's talent and desire to be better but didn't know how to help him. He paid for private batting lessons and saw that Gavin was focused and engaged during the lessons, but he wouldn't practice at home. When he would ask Gavin to practice, he often did not want to, or he was busy doing other things. Gavin and his father decided to set goals and create routines with those goals in mind using these five questions:

1. **WHAT IS YOUR LONG-TERM GOAL?**

   Gavin's long-term goal was to get a college scholarship in base-ball. That's an awesome goal, but he had about six years left until college. For kids ages 10 to 12, try to keep the long-term goals from three to six months out so you can practice assessing progress and measuring success with your child. For Gavin, this goal may be to finish his next season with a specific batting average, or to make a special select team in a tryout that is four months away.

2. **WHAT ARE DAILY AND WEEKLY THINGS THAT YOU CAN DO TO REACH THIS GOAL?**

   Gavin needed to improve his batting average in the spring base-ball season. He could do drills in his backyard by himself daily for 15 minutes. He could go to lessons with his father twice a week, and do some strength training three times a week.

3. **WHAT ARE POTENTIAL ROADBLOCKS THAT CAN GET IN THE WAY OF REACHING YOUR GOAL?**

   By asking this question, Gavin's dad learned that Gavin avoided practicing because the only time he could play online games with his friends was when his father typically asked him to practice with him. He also found that he often asked Gavin to practice when he still had schoolwork to do. Knowing this, they could create a more sustainable routine that kept Gavin's needs in mind.

4. **HOW CAN YOU MEASURE YOUR GOAL?**

   To track Gavin's weekly progress, they agreed that a successful week would mean meeting five of the six scheduled activities (drills, training, and lessons). If Gavin didn't follow his routine, they'd discuss what happened at the end of the week and what led him to miss an activity.

5. **HOW CAN YOU REWARD YOURSELF FOR SHORT-TERM SUCCESSES TOWARD THE LONG-TERM GOAL?**

   If Gavin had a successful week, he would reward himself with extra free time to relax on Sunday.

After the season was over, Gavin was able to raise his batting average by 50 points! Later in the fall, he was able to use the same tactics to raise his grades—even though it was something he was less passionate about than baseball.

Use SMART Goals

When developing goals, make sure they are SMART: Specific, Measurable, Attainable, Relevant, and Time-Based.

For children with ADHD, it's important they learn that their goals should follow this template. For example, many children with ADHD want to achieve better grades, which is a great goal to have, but it's not specific or measurable. You might help them change this goal to something as simple as "I want to make A's and B's this semester in math and reading," which is both specific enough and time-based.

Sometimes, children with ADHD can be a little ambitious and create goals that are not attainable. If your 10-year-old is failing in a few subjects and sets the goal of making all A's this semester, you may need to help her understand that the process of getting to all A's may take time. It's also important that the child's goals and routines be relevant to their desires and the future.

A key step that many children and adults with ADHD skip when it comes to setting goals is the time-based part. If there is no time limit to measure success, they will be less likely to follow through with routines. Taking time to reflect on the effectiveness of the routines that you establish with your family is an important process for you as a parent. It's also important for the child to learn to evaluate and measure how well a new routine is working for them.

Sticking to Routines

Once you and your child have agreed to a daily or weekly routine, it's time to start following it. Here are some specific strategies to help your kids remember and stick to the routines they've committed to. You'll learn how to enforce routines while still leaving room for some autonomy and flexibility.

Keep It Simple

One of the struggles I see with many parents in my practice is that they overschedule their children or create a rigid routine without any flexibility or time for the child to manage themselves. Children who are not allowed time to make their own decisions can become easily bored, stressed, and overly dependent on their parents.

To avoid these consequences, keep the routines simple and age-appropriate. A good rule of thumb is to give one chore or activity per year of age for a daily routine, and no more than seven activities for a given time of day (morning or evening) for any age. For example, your 4-year-old may have a visual chart for the afternoon with pictures representing an after-school routine of four activities: playtime, dinner, bath, and getting ready for bed.

With older children you may add more activities, but you'll still want to keep to the limit of seven. Any more than that would be overwhelming for a child with ADHD and executive functioning issues, but would also set yourself up for failure.

If your daily and weekly routines do not include time for free play or family time, you may want to find a way to integrate those things into the routine. In her book *The Self-Esteem Trap*, clinical psychologist Polly Young-Eisendrath contends that parents who overschedule their child before the age of 11 or 12 may be distracting from their natural development. Overscheduling robs them of developing ways of keeping themselves busy and entertained, fostering social interaction with the family, and developing a sense of independence. Although it's good to have routines and scheduled activities for children, free playtime and family time are even more important. Scheduled activities can be enriching, but should not be the sole focus of weekly routines. A balance is best.

Prep Them for What's Next

Transitioning from one activity to another can be exceedingly difficult for children with ADHD and executive functioning issues. Perhaps the child is exhausted at the end of the day because they are mentally drained from school. Maybe they are overly focused on whatever has their attention at the moment or they have difficulty managing their time and anticipating what is next. No matter the reason, it is important to help them know what's next.

If you are developing a new routine, simply ask your child what is next. Let's say your 5-year-old is taking a bath. You may ask two to three minutes before bath time is over, "What do you think we are going to do after the bath?" Asking the question rather than simply stating what comes next is important, because it forces them to retrieve information. It also helps them accept that change is coming. This ensures that they have heard your message and are somewhat prepared for the transition.

Let's say your older child is in the middle of building a huge castle in an online game. You may first want to enter her world before reminding her of the transition. If she's supposed to be coming down for dinner soon, try to come in and sit next to her, comment on the game, or put your hand on her shoulder. Gradually engaging her before the warning of the transition can prep her for the transition more effectively than abruptly yelling, "Five more minutes!"

Remember Your Priorities

Children with ADHD and executive functioning deficits may take a while to learn and follow new habits and routines. This lag can create frustration and power struggles between parents and children. If a parent expects their child to adhere to a routine or schedule in a demanding and rigid way, that parent is inviting conflict, especially with a child with ADHD. As a parent, it can really help to remember priorities when it comes to routines.

Let's say your 10-year-old with a diagnosis of ADHD and autism spectrum disorder is consistently able to follow your evening routine listed here:

3:30 p.m. to 4:30 p.m. – free time

4:30 p.m. to 6 p.m. – schoolwork

6:00 p.m. to 6:30 p.m. – family dinner time

6:30 p.m. to 7 p.m. – family game time/TV

7 p.m. to 7:15 p.m. – shower, brush teeth, prepare for next day

7:15 p.m. to 8 p.m. – free time/relax in room

Now let's say he is on top of every part of this routine except for shower time and brushing his teeth. Because of his inability to manage his time, he rarely does these tasks within 15 minutes, and then there is frustration that he does not get as much time to relax afterward. If he's only behind by a few minutes, ask yourself if the few minutes are worth the struggle. If it is an issue to you, help brainstorm with him to figure out how he can be more efficient showering and brushing his teeth. If it's not, then allow him to have his free time as long as he is meeting the timeline within reason.

Children with ADHD and executive functioning issues need structure, but they also need flexibility. Being rigid or authoritarian with routines can only increase anxiety and pushback. Decide which parts of the routine you want to prioritize over others. If the child is a little behind in school but generally falls to sleep as soon as his head hits the pillow, then you may choose to be a little more rigid with the study time than the bedtime. When creating your family's routines and schedules, staying flexible will help everyone avoid unnecessary stress. Remember the authoritative parents we mentioned in part 1 of the book. You want structure with the important things, and flexibility when appropriate—and when your child needs it.

School Support

Most successful teachers use classroom routines to create a predictable environment for learning. Why not borrow their expertise when developing your own routines?

For example, if your child is struggling with homework after school, ask your child's teacher how much time is expected to complete a homework assignment. If they expect that your 7-year-old should be spending no more than 30 minutes on homework but your child is spending two hours finishing the work, they may agree to adjust the amount of homework for your child, which can eliminate a lot of struggle in your evening routine.

For older children who have multiple teachers and rotate from classroom to classroom, you may want to ask each teacher how much time is to be expected for independent study outside of homework. Doing so can help you determine how much time you need to set aside for schoolwork every day.

If homework takes an excessive amount of time, you can talk to the teacher about the possibility of limiting their homework to every other problem or allowing the student to type answers. If forgetfulness is an issue, perhaps the teacher can offer a second textbook to be kept at home. The teacher might also agree to "chunk" in-class assignments, such as saying, "Do the first 10 problems, then come see me."

What to Avoid

For children with ADHD, a school day can be exhausting. It's filled with transitions, demands to focus on unstimulating ideas, and a constant need for impulse control. It takes more mental energy for them to get through the day than for a neurotypical child.

When developing an afternoon and evening routine for your children, you won't want to expect them to jump into mentally taxing activities like homework or chores right after school. If your child takes stimulant medication for ADHD, there may be a "coming-down" period at the end of the day when it's even more difficult for them to focus, and they may be moody.

You know your child best, so find their sweet spot between right after school and the "coming-down" period. Use this time to allow them to have a period of free time or a small snack right after school, so they can replenish their mental energy. Ideally, this time would also involve some sort of exercise or physical activity. Schedule homework time so they have plenty of time to finish the work.

Make It Fun!

Children with ADHD are curious and often drawn to new concepts and learning new things. You can add a little fun and variety to your child's daily routine using "Wild Cards." One "Wild Card" can say that on rainy days your child can pick a new activity from a hat that they've never tried before. Some activities might be creating a small volcano with baking soda and vinegar, doing an online yoga class, or trying an online origami tutorial.

For transitions, you can play their favorite song as a reminder to move on to the next activity. It's simple, but it makes things a little different and personalized, getting the child to buy into the routine. The trick is to keep coming up with new ideas, as new things can get old real fast for children with ADHD.

Pro Tip

Realistic and flexible are two key goals when creating new daily routines. Instead of expecting a child with executive functioning issues to hit the ground running, you might aim for 70 percent compliance the first week. Maybe this means your child can transition from one activity to another with only one reminder and without defiance. Once you've achieved 70 percent compliance, you can work toward gradual improvement.

As mentioned on page 118, research states you can expect a new behavior to become automatic in 66 days, but that doesn't take one's level of executive functioning into account. I encourage you to be patient with the process of teaching your child to create and establish new routines. If it does not work the first time, that doesn't mean you have to give up. Have a discussion with your child about why it didn't work and try to adapt accordingly. Just the very act of talking with them about daily routines teaches them the importance of predictability and structure. Open dialogue empowers them to speak assertively, and to become aware of what works for them and what does not so they can start to take charge of their own growth. And by listening to them, you'll learn valuable information!

Staying Focused at Home and in Class

One of the core characteristics of ADHD is difficulty maintaining focus in the classroom. Dr. Barton Schmitt, author of *My Child Is Sick!*, states that a typically developing child should be able to focus and maintain attention for three to five minutes per year of age, starting at age 2. That means you can expect a typical 4-year-old child to focus on a task for 12 to 20 minutes. Children with ADHD and executive functioning deficits may not be able to meet that expectation—but you can help! In this chapter, you'll learn how your child can practice staying focused at home, which will help them perform better in class. You'll also get tips on how to engage teachers to accommodate your child's needs in the classroom.

Set Them Up for Success

Through a combination of parent training, effective classroom management by teachers, and targeted activities, you can see a marked improvement in your child's ability to maintain focus in the classroom. Let's start with general strategies you can implement at home to build a good foundation for more sophisticated skills.

Use Playtime to Stretch Attention Span

According to Dr. Schmitt, a 5-year-old child needs to be able to maintain attention for at least 15 minutes to be able to succeed in school. For many children with ADHD, 15 minutes of continuous focus can be really difficult at first.

For younger children around ages 4 to 7, start extending their ability by encouraging them to focus on playful and imaginative tasks. In a 2016 study, researchers noted a positive relationship between play therapy and growth in attention span. Working with a play therapist can help develop a stronger and longer-lasting attention span.

If play therapy is not an option, you can initiate a simple playtime with your child that incorporates some basic principles of play therapy. This playtime would ideally include a variety of toys that allow them to incorporate imaginative play, such as a play doctor's kit, play food, dress-up toys, puppets, and more. During this 20- to 30-minute playtime, try to adhere to three guidelines:

LET YOUR CHILD LEAD – You want your child to use their imagination. Suggesting activities or guiding them in play can be detrimental—you don't want to limit their choices or expressions. Encourage them to make decisions and direct their own playtime, as long as they are being safe with toys or materials.

STAY AWAY FROM QUESTIONS – Asking too many questions may take away from imaginative time because the child feels the need to respond. Keep playtime focused on your child, not about what you want to know. You can always ask questions later.

FOCUS ON STRENGTHS, NOT WEAKNESSES – Pay attention to what the child is doing and what they want to achieve from their playtime. Mirror your child's actions with your words. You may sound like a narrator at times, but that's okay. This may sound like, "You are feeling really proud when you put on that superhero costume," or "You are taking such good care of me by giving me that toy medicine." Saying this helps the child know that you are engaged, which encourages prolonged focus.

Although this advice can be helpful, playtime is not an equal substitute for play therapy. A trained play therapist can help with your child's attention span in concrete ways. Many play therapists are also trained in filial therapy, which helps parents develop play therapy techniques by enabling them to work with the child under the therapist's supervision. Even if you are not able to engage in play therapy or filial therapy, these simple tips can create an environment for sustained focus and shared attention. In time, you may notice that your child is displaying more focus in their play and attending to their imaginative stories for longer and longer periods of time.

Create an Inattention Profile

Most children with ADHD and executive functioning difficulties don't know what paying attention looks like. In fact, they rarely have the opportunity to think about their own inattention, except when they are getting scolded in school or at home. You can help them identify some of their inattention triggers and brainstorm how to use their environment as reminders to focus on the task at hand. This next strategy works best with children ages 8 and up, as younger children may not have the ability to reflect on their thinking in moments of inattention.

Recently, I met with a new 12-year-old client whom we will call Dylan. Dylan was diagnosed with ADHD about two years ago. He has struggled with his schoolwork since moving to 6th grade, where he's expected to focus and attend to more lectures than in elementary school. After speaking with Dylan's parents, psychiatrist, and one of his teachers, I met with him. He immediately struck me as a generally happy and affable young guy who liked Star Wars. However, in our first session, I was forced to repeat questions several times, as he was fascinated and distracted by the pictures on my wall and the small puzzles that I had on my desk. As we talked, he expressed frustration with school and not being able to remember what teachers said.

Like many children with ADHD, Dylan seemed to lack awareness of how ADHD has affected his life. To help children like Dylan understand themselves when they are having difficulty focusing, you can ask the following questions:

→ Is there a time of day or a class that is most difficult to focus in?
→ When you catch yourself not focusing, what are you thinking about most of the time?

→ Is there anything about the classroom itself or the other students or teachers that is distracting?

→ Is there anything that you tell yourself or do that helps you focus?

These questions help gauge where a child's mind is when they are about to lose focus. The goal is not to force them to focus more intently. The goal is to help them catch themselves more quickly when losing focus, so they can hear and retain more information.

Using Dylan's answers, we developed an "Inattention Profile" that he could take to class as a physical reminder to catch himself from losing focus. The Inattention Profile is simply a small piece of paper with pictures of the child's biggest sources of distraction and motivation. You want this paper to be large enough to fit the visuals needed, but small enough to be able to keep in a binder. In Dylan's profile, we put a picture of athletes playing sports and video games since those were what he listed as his biggest distractors. We also put a picture of his favorite college's mascot, as he said that getting into that school motivates him to focus more.

Since Dylan said his math class in the morning was the most difficult class to pay attention in, I asked his math teacher to remind Dylan to use his Inattention Profile daily and have it out on his desk during lecture or review time. At the end of each class, Dylan would give himself a letter grade for how well the profile worked for him and how well he focused in class. After school, his parents would ask him, "What grade did you give yourself?" Asking this helped him reflect on using the profile so he could continue to remember it.

In the beginning, Dylan's self-report was full of C's, but after talking about it and getting nonjudgmental reminders from his teacher, he began self-reporting A's. I coordinated with his teacher to arrange for preferential seating away from the window, where the view of a basketball hoop often distracts him. We also discussed new distractions in class in therapy sessions with Dylan and tips for appropriate note-taking. I recommended that he use a template from the teacher for note-taking, with some blanks to fill out so he could write enough to enhance his ability to remember the information, but not so much that he would miss instruction. By the end of the year, Dylan's grades improved significantly.

The time we devoted to reflecting on his distractions made him much more aware—he even began to advocate for changes at home to make sure his environment was free from distractions. Although the "Inattention Profile" sounds like a simple concept, visual representations of distractors and motivators can have a powerful effect on kids when they're losing focus. Most importantly, it's a less invasive way to help empower kids to manage their own attention.

A Dose of Nature

It may seem strange to say that leaving the classroom can help with focus in the classroom, but a study from the University of Illinois at Urbana-Champaign noted that spending time in nature can actually improve kids' focus and attention. The researchers found that children with a diagnosis of ADHD concentrate better after a 20- to 30-minute walk in nature compared to walks in an urban or suburban area. It was noted that they couldn't pinpoint what it was about the park setting that caused the improved focus and attention span, whether it was the greenery or general lack of buildings, but that there was a significant positive relationship between attention span and being outside in nature.

Dr. David Nowell, a neurologist and international speaker regarding ADHD, theorized that being outdoors and in nature provides an opportunity to practice "soft fascination," or a focus on something that is moderately stimulating but does not overwhelm the senses. Being outside, for example, provides an environment of constant change. With every step you take, the scenery changes. You hear different sounds and smell different scents. But these changes occur gradually, and they are not overstimulating. This setting provides a soothing environment where children can practice blocking out stimulation that is easier to filter out than more difficult distractors, like other children talking or a loud bell chiming every hour.

Although you may not be able to convince your school district to teach outdoors in parks, you can integrate this "green time" into your own family routines. If you live near a park, you can invite your child to go on a walk with you before homework time. If you don't live near nature, you can set aside green time for Sunday afternoons before the school week and drive somewhere to go on a nature walk with the family.

Boosting Focus

In this section, we'll explore more specific strategies for handling your child's inattention at home and in the classroom. By working with teachers and adapting your home environment, you can create additional opportunities for your child to stay focused and on task at home and in the classroom.

Adapt to Your Child's Needs

When I was a 4th grade teacher, I loved decorating my classroom. During my last year of teaching, I created a room that had a jungle theme with a life-size cardboard tree in the corner of the room complete with charts and pictures filling every space of the walls.

Little did I know, I was setting some of my students up for failure with overstimulating classroom decorations. I remember one student in particular who was constantly leaving his seat to read one of my charts that showed a list of reptiles and always craning his neck around to look at the clownfish in the fish tank. I learned that it's so important that teachers and parents adjust the learning environment for children with attention issues to minimize distractions.

According to researchers at Carnegie Mellon University, children who learned in highly decorated classrooms were more easily distracted, spent more time off task, and demonstrated smaller learning gains than when the distracting decorations were removed. The study tested children of all abilities and did not account for ADHD or children with difficulty paying attention. It is reasonable to assume that children with ADHD or issues with focus and attention may be affected even more significantly by distractors in the classroom.

The researchers don't suggest taking down all the displays, but instead propose that teachers decorate their classrooms with children's attentional abilities in mind. Looking back with this knowledge, I would have taken down all decorations near the front of the class where I stood and where students would have to focus their attention. I would have focused my decorations on teaching tools. That said, you may not be able to convince a teacher to change their classroom décor, but you can request preferential seating for your child away from distractors.

To create a good homework area for children with ADHD or executive functioning issues, test out these simple strategies:

REMOVE DISTRACTIONS – Find a space with very few pictures on the walls and little to no unnecessary sounds. Choose somewhere quiet, away from the high-traffic areas of the house.

HAVE EVERYTHING IN EASY REACH – Make sure your child has what they need in this area, like paper, pencils, markers, calculator, and so on. This leads to fewer disruptive breaks to stand up and get materials, which inevitably leads to more distractions.

SET THE RIGHT AMBIENCE – Experiment with temperature and light. According to a study at the University of Cologne, students concentrated better under natural light as compared to fluorescent light, so it may be good to have a study area by the window to let in natural light.

Although you can't totally control your child's learning environment in school, you can ensure your child's workspace at home is free from distractions to instill good habits.

Check in Gently

When children with ADHD try to do work at home, parents may either leave them completely to their own devices or constantly look over their shoulders, becoming more of a distraction than a supporter. Finding the right balance of checking in often enough to help them maintain focus without giving them the impression that you don't believe they can focus on their own is tricky!

To support your child during homework time, create a game plan on when and how you will check in. First, remember that a typically developing child can focus on a task for three to five times their age. To be safe, let's use a multiple of two. So, if your 8-year-old child is doing homework alone on a subject that he grasps and understands, you may want to check in every 16 minutes or so. Of course, you can adapt this timing according to your needs, but it's a good place to start when deciding how often to check in on your child.

Now that you know how often to check in, what to say? You'll want to approach them in a way that you're not too much of a distraction and you allow them time to try focusing independently. A simple rule of thumb is to use as few words as possible. You can knock on the door and say, "I'm just checking in," or "Need any help?" If they answer "no," and you can see that they have made progress on their work, they can continue.

If your child is younger than 8 or new to school and homework, they may need more frequent check-ins. You may even need to do homework with them depending on their age and knowledge of the topic, but if they are capable of attending to homework by themselves, it's always good to get them to try.

We never want to do something for the child that the child can already do.

To know if a child is capable of attending to their homework, I like to think of the "Million Dollar Question," meaning that if a genie were to give them a million dollars to focus on their homework for a certain amount of time, could they potentially do it for that amount of time? This question can help you determine what they are capable of doing, so you can set appropriate expectations.

Some Fidgeting Can Be Good!

Many parents and schools advocate for the use of fidgets, or small handheld items that a child can squeeze or manipulate that aren't too distracting in the classroom. In his book *Spark*, Dr. John Ratey notes that physical activity as small as fidgeting with hands increases the neurotransmitters norepinephrine and dopamine in similar ways as stimulant medications. Both of those chemicals play key roles in rewarding focus and attention in our brains. This helps explain why it is good for children with ADHD to move while they learn.

Purdue University professor Sydney S. Zentall explains that doing two things at once for the ADHD brain can enhance performance and focus on a primary task. The trick is that the secondary task must not be as cognitively difficult or a significant distractor. In other words, it must be something that the child can do without thinking too much about it. For example, for a primary task of doing homework or studying for a test, the secondary task can be using a fidget or bouncing lightly on an exercise ball. If the secondary task is a puzzle that is difficult to solve or a fancy new fidget spinner that demands a child's attention, then using that secondary task can take away from the child's ability to focus.

Here are some secondary task activities that can be beneficial:

→ Doodling (not drawing a complete picture, just doodling shapes)
→ Using a strong exercise band between the legs of a desk and repetitively bouncing or kicking it
→ Bouncing on an exercise ball instead of sitting in a chair
→ Using a squeeze ball or touching something soft taped under their desk
→ Chewing gum

Try introducing these techniques one at time, and then check in with your child to see which seems most helpful.

School Support

The most important thing parents need to know when addressing their child's lack of focus or attention in the classroom is your rights, so you can advocate for your child's right to learn with appropriate support in place. Most schools and educators genuinely want to help. But things can slip through the cracks, as schools have to cater to so many different children. To help your child, it's necessary to be proactive and get comfortable with the process of requesting accommodations.

One great resource in this area is the CHADD (Children and Adults with Attention-Deficit/Hyperactivity Disorder) website (see Resources, page 181), which has a section called "Know Your Rights" with a link to the United States Department of Education Office for Civil Rights. This document gives parents information on how schools use a Section 504 plan to make sure that a child with ADHD can be accommodated for in the classroom, and on the parents' rights in the process of enacting a 504 plan.

A 504 plan is an agreement between the school and parents to accommodate a child's disability and give the child "an even playing field." Having a 504 plan in place for your child with ADHD and executive functioning issues can provide them with the in-class accommodations they need to succeed. It can also give you greater insight into what's working for your child and hopefully help you appropriately engage your child at home, as a result of increased parent-teacher communication and a better understanding of how the teacher is accommodating your child's needs.

Getting a 504 enacted for your child typically starts by meeting with the child's teacher and counselor. Sometimes an outside psychologist or neurologist can strengthen the case for a 504 by providing a diagnosis. If necessary, CHADD can also help, as they have attorneys who specialize in the educational welfare of children.

What to Avoid

As parents, we sometimes want immediate answers. Instead of demanding answers right away, give the child a few extra seconds to respond. Many parents who do not have ADHD may be able to process information and focus more effectively than their children. This creates a dynamic in which the child struggles to focus on a conversation as the parent is whizzing along faster than they can handle. If you know that you process information and speak at a faster rate than most, and if your child has difficulty with focus and attention, do your best to slow down. By slowing down and being patient, you are giving them time to process what you are saying and formulate a response.

Make It Fun!

Next time you play a board game, try adding some fun distractions to help your child practice filtering out distracting stimulation. This may include playing distracting music or doing a silly, distracting dance during a game of Connect Four or Memory that requires focus.

Another idea is to have a weekly challenge doing something new. It should be something that is completely out of your child's skill set that requires focus and careful attention. Examples could be drawing a picture with your nondominant hand or blindfolded, picking up small things with your feet, or saying the alphabet backward.

These kinds of activities alone, although fun, may not help your child focus in the classroom. But talking with your child about how they managed to ignore distractions during or after the game can help. Discussions like these help them become aware of strategies that they are adapting without even knowing it, and remind them to use these strategies in the future.

Knowing my ADHD diagnosis, I have learned the best sequence in which to work. If I need to focus on a project that I can control, like writing reports or notes, planning for marketing meetings, or simply answering e-mails, I always start off with the easiest and quickest task and then delve into the most difficult task that requires the most focus and attention. This way, I get some positive momentum and my brain ready for more taxing work without tiring it out. I also know that certain times of day work better for me. If I am going to have to focus on something that demands a lot of mental energy, I make sure to plan to do it in the mid- to late morning if possible.

A two-year global study by a project management software company found that, across the globe, people displayed the best and most intense concentration at around 11 a.m. This is certainly the case for me, as I feel depleted late in the afternoon. I can't say personally when is the best time for your child with ADHD to focus, but it is good for you to ask the question and figure out when may be the time of day that their brains are the most efficient.

If you are able to adjust your child's schedule to have the most difficult class around this time of day, you may see some improvement in focus and attention. Obviously, that's not always possible, and if you cannot change your child's schedule, start teaching your child the process of starting out their homework with something easy and quick and then diving into something more difficult. Discover more about them and how they learn so that you can teach them about themselves.

Managing Time Wisely

Time management is a crucial life skill at all stages of development. It requires the ability to delay gratification, prioritize certain activities over others to meet a goal, and self-regulate. Children with ADHD and executive functioning weaknesses often struggle with managing their time, which can lead to anxiety and stress. But when children learn to plan even a few minutes ahead, they can better prioritize and manage their time. Children as young as 4 years old can manage their time in play if given a visual representation of the amount of time they have available to them. In this chapter, you'll learn how to help your child build and practice time management skills by helping them break down large projects, more accurately estimate time, and understand and work through procrastination.

Set Them Up for Success

Look at a lack of time management not as a character flaw, but as a sign of an underdeveloped skill you can help your child learn. Mastering this skill can lead your child to feel less anxiety and a greater sense of control. Here are some general strategies you can start implementing right now.

Plan According to Ability

Let's take stock of your child's current ability to think ahead. In her presentation "Executive Functions and ADHD in Children," ADHD coach Cindy Goldrich recommends using the following guidelines to help your child plan in line with what they are capable of:

AGE	PLANNING ABILITY
2 years old	Now
3 to 5 years old	5 to 20 minutes
6 and 7 years old	Several hours
8 to 11 years old	8 to 12 hours
12 to 16 years old	2 to 3 days

With younger children, you can practice time management during playtime. For example, you and your 5-year-old can talk using these three questions:

→ What's the most important activity or your favorite activity during playtime?

→ How are we going to measure the time we have (such as with a clock; a colored, sand, or analog timer; warnings; the amount of time it takes to play five songs)?

→ Are there any things that might take up a lot of time besides the most important activity?

Guiding children through these questions can help them prioritize and manage their time. It also helps them learn to account for their time. With any child, you'll want to give reminders of time when they are playing. This may simply sound like, "You have five more minutes of playtime." Reminders help prepare their brain for a transition.

With children ages 8 to 10, you can help them plan further out than just a few minutes ahead. For example, if your 8-year-old son can potentially plan for up to eight hours, then you can invite him to help plan out a day of activities on a weekend trip. You might ask these questions when discussing the trip:

→ How much time are we going to have on our trip?
→ What is the most important thing you want to do while we are camping?
→ How much time will we need to devote to this?
→ What are the things we need to do to make sure we survive, and how much time will they take?
→ Are there any things that may take up more time than we have available?
→ How are we going to measure our time?

These examples show that breaking down big things doesn't have to start with large school projects. Use fun activities to get kids familiar with the process. This strategy can prepare them for planning ahead for less-fun tasks like essays and school presentations.

Break Down Long-Term Tasks

Many children with ADHD and executive functioning weaknesses may spend time on unproductive activities. This diversion can be a way to avoid the stress and overwhelming feeling involved with tasks that require long-term planning or time management. When presented with a list of chores or expectations for a book report by a certain deadline, children with ADHD may feel anxiety, because taking in all of that information and breaking it down into achievable goals can seem overwhelming, if not impossible. Instead of planning ways to manage their time, these children may choose to wait until the last minute and then rush through the work, and as a result do not perform to their potential.

I recently met with a 12-year-old student we will call Ally. Ally often would procrastinate with homework and rush to complete it at the last minute, causing stress to herself and her mom in the process. Ally was in honors courses and did well on tests, but with long-term projects and homework, she was constantly in a rush and, as a result, made simple mistakes. Consequently, she was consistently making B's and C's instead of the A's she was capable of.

Ally's mom assumed that work wasn't important to Ally—after all, if it was, she would be able to do it. Since Ally was in honors classes, she was clearly capable of doing the work. Ally's mom did not understand that despite her obvious intelligence, planning and prioritizing work was a skill that did not come naturally to her. These skills had to be taught.

I sat down with Ally and made a list of what she had to do to prepare for her upcoming test in a week. Ally rated each item on the list based on the difficulty and the necessity of each task. She then estimated the amount of time needed to finish each task. It looked something like this:

	DIFFICULTY	TIME NEEDED
READ/HIGHLIGHT CHAPTERS	2	2 hours
BUY FLASH CARDS	1	15 minutes
MAKE FLASH CARDS	1	1 hour
STUDY FLASH CARDS	3	2 hours
HAVE MOM QUIZ ME	4	1 hour

When we added up the number of hours studying would take, it came to 6 hours and 15 minutes. To a child with ADHD, that probably seems like an eternity. I asked Ally how she felt about six-plus hours of work, and she answered that she felt frustrated and anxious. But then I asked how she felt about studying for the test for less than an hour each day. She did not feel excited, but she felt much less anxious.

Like Ally, when a child with ADHD or executive functioning issues avoids tasks, they are seeing the task as one big problem. You can help them break it down into smaller pieces and show them that a little work every day can feel less stressful than all of the work at once when you write it down on paper.

Using Ally's list, we created a weekly plan that ensured she would not spend more than one and a half hours studying in one sitting. We then jotted it down on a weekly calendar, accounting for other schoolwork and her activities. We also discussed which tasks needed intense focus and which did not. Making flash cards didn't require intense focus, so her mom agreed that Ally could make them while watching a show if her mom was able to check on her progress. Ally also checked in with her mom after each task was completed.

By mapping out the difficulty level and amount of time needed for each step, Ally felt more motivated. The following week, Ally was able to study for the test without putting it off to the last minute, which led to less frustration for everyone—and it helped her score better on the test than she had in previous tests in the class and led to her earning some well-deserved ice cream and movies that Friday night!

Practice Estimating Time

The internal clock of children with ADHD and executive functioning skill deficits is a little different than in other people. A 2017 study by *European Child & Adolescent Psychiatry* found "deficits in time perception and processing speed in children and adolescents with ADHD," and that there was a link between correct time estimation and processing speed. This finding may help explain why, when you tell your child they have 10 minutes left to play video games, it feels like three minutes to them. The car ride to Grandma's house that takes 30 minutes might feel like three hours to your 8-year-old with ADHD. Teaching kids how to estimate time accurately can be a key component in helping them learn to manage their time.

To help children ages 7 and under estimate time more effectively, simply talk out loud more about time. You may say, "It was 8:09 a.m. when we left for school, and it is 8:19 a.m. now. It took us 10 minutes to get to school." Doing so helps them pay attention to what 10 minutes feels like in the moment, so they can use that experience to estimate time more accurately in the future. Be sure to round up or down to 15 minutes, 30 minutes, or an hour rather than saying the exact minutes, like 17 or 43 minutes. Rounding will get them familiar to the most commonly used measurements of time.

With children ages 8 and up, you can talk more often about how much time an activity takes. Use technology to help them measure time. If they have homework, have them estimate how much time it will take, then set an alarm. They don't need to rush to beat the alarm. The goal is to get better at estimating the time, so after they estimate the time, they do their work without a clock nearby to pressure them to finish in a certain time. Afterward, they can review with you how close they were in their estimate, and then review how close they have been in other recent attempts.

Another key part of managing time for a child with ADHD is to understand where they get lost in time. Usually, this moment is when they are so focused on something that they forget what is going on around them. Make a list of these activities and call them "Time Travel Activities," or something that appeals to your child. Make sure they have a way to measure their time when they're engaging in these fun "Time Travel Activities" so they can learn how long they really took. The key here is just to help them be aware of their inaccurate estimates of time and when they are the most inaccurate, which is probably during an activity they enjoy.

Handling Procrastination

In my practice, procrastination is one of the most significant roadblocks for many college students and young adults in their 20s on their pathway to success. It's important to understand why procrastination happens and address it at as young an age as possible to prevent habits from being harder to break.

There are two main types of procrastinators: active procrastinators and passive procrastinators. The active procrastinator is the one who thrives under pressure and is "procrastinating with a plan." They are typically cool, calm, and collected. With a generally easygoing temperament, they are confident they will meet their goals, even despite their procrastination. They may feel more creative and find the rush of finishing a project last-minute exhilarating.

Passive procrastinators, on the other hand, are those who just put off things to avoid stress. They often feel overwhelmed by projects and are more pessimistic about their performance. These are the procrastinators who need help.

The key to helping a passive procrastinator is to reduce their anxiety regarding certain projects. If you've already tried to address their anxiety by breaking down the problem into smaller tasks and prioritizing work and they still can't get started, try the following:

SEPARATE PERFORMANCE FROM SELF-WORTH – Focus on your child's effort and not the result. Give rewards or positive feedback for the time they put in and strategies they used, rather than their grade.

LINK THE TASK TO A DESIRED EMOTION – Remind your child of the times when they felt proud of planning ahead for a task or the relief they will feel when the job is done. We are all motivated by our emotions, so help them feel the positive effects of their effort!

EMPATHIZE WITH THEIR SENSE OF BEING OVERWHELMED – Talk to your child about when you felt anxious about a big presentation or overwhelmed before a big test. That normalizes their feelings, and they're more likely to listen to your advice when they know you've been there.

MANAGE PERFECTIONISM – Your child may need your help realizing that perfection is not possible. Ask them if they expect others to be perfect. If not, then ask them to be fair to themselves. Help them understand realistic expectations for assignments and overall grades, and that doing their best is what counts.

Help Them Measure Time

As we've explored, children with ADHD often have trouble accurately estimating the amount of time that an activity will take. This struggle is hard for many adults to relate to, especially those without executive functioning deficits. If a parent does not understand that their child has difficulty internally measuring time, then naturally they will give the child time limits or expectations that they will consistently fail to meet.

For any child with ADHD, any expectation of time needs to come with a way to measure that amount of time. For younger children who have not mastered telling time on a clock, you might use a colored timer that changes colors as time counts down, giving children the clue that time is almost up.

This strategy is important not just for younger children, but for older kids as well. If your 10-year-old often loses track of time while he is playing games online, get him a digital clock and put it directly in front of his monitor or TV. By doing so, you have at least given him a way to measure his time.

Change the Narrative

Many passive procrastinators can be perfectionists who create unrealistic expectations for themselves and therefore avoid difficult work. Some children with ADHD or executive functioning issues also do not see the value in a difficult task, because it's not immediately rewarding to them. Others may assume that they can't complete even a doable task as a result of past failures, and therefore give up before trying. You can help your child challenge negative thoughts that lead to passive procrastination and create new work habits.

For the perfectionist child, you'll want to help them break their "all-or-nothing" mindset and learn to create fair expectations for themselves. To work on the all-or-nothing mindset, discuss how success in a project or activity can be measured in many ways. For example, you can create a rating scale for measuring success from many different perspectives. Instead of just measuring success on the final grade, come up with your own rating scale to let them measure how successful they were at an assignment or task. It can look something like this:

Rate how true this statement is between 1 and 5, with 5 being the truest.

- → I had fun doing this project.
- → I learned something valuable while completing this project.
- → I am proud of the effort that I put in.
- → I am satisfied with my final grade.
- → I will have to do projects like this in the future.

Just the simple act of rating these different categories helps kids see that there are other ways of measuring success, rather than just a single grade.

For the child with ADHD who cannot see the value in a task, you can help them see how completing the task may lead them to feel an emotion they like or less of an emotion they don't like. With children ages 7 or younger, mention how relieved they will feel when they are done with their spelling words, or how proud they will feel when they finish cleaning their room so their friends can come over to play. With kids ages 8 and older, mention how this task leads to things that they want. This may sound like, "If you wash the dishes now, you'll be done with your chores and can watch a movie without interruption." You are motivating them to get started on tasks more quickly by focusing on the benefit.

The child who feels defeated before they even start a task or project will need a lot of incremental encouragement—that is, boosts along the way. For example, if your child struggles to get ready for school after breakfast and they beat themselves up daily because they can't get ready in time, lead them throughout the process with bits of encouragement. This may sound like, "Good job getting your clothes on, now it's time to get your books," or "You are really on time with getting showered—four minutes ahead of yesterday! I bet we can be on time today." These small bits of positive feedback remind them that they are on task and what's next without shame or distress.

School Support

Schools use different interventions to help children with ADHD and executive functioning difficulties manage their time more efficiently. One of the simplest things that works in elementary classrooms are visual schedules that list the day's activities. Most teachers just write the schedule on the board, so children can visually see the sequence of activities and then hopefully internalize the schedule. Some teachers may even engage the class in estimating how much time would be needed for certain activities.

For older children, time management needs to be more self-directed than with elementary school students. Your 10- and 12-year-olds with ADHD and executive functioning issues are consistently expected to manage their time, prioritize, and use their short-term memory. For many preteens I work with, the biggest difficulty is switching classes. If your preteen struggles with transitions, ask if your child can leave their classes a few minutes early so they can transition from one class to another with a little extra time, or work with them to make a plan for transitions between bells, such as making sure they have all their books if their locker is too far away to return to between classes. This is a simple way to relieve stress and make sure they have everything they need.

What to Avoid

Although many adults with ADHD can be good multitaskers, you may want to think twice about letting your child do many different tasks at once.

ADHD coach Cindy Goldrich explains that children with ADHD cannot multitask two tasks that demand focus, but they may be able to multitask if one of the activities is routine to them. This is where that fidget or secondary prop can help the child focus on the primary subject of focus. In this case, they may not be able to watch a new episode of their favorite show while studying, but they might be able to listen to familiar music while studying.

Keep in mind that people with ADHD are often forced to multitask due to procrastination or inaccurate estimations of time. To instill good time management habits, you can remind your child that trying to do two things at once may take up more time than focusing on one task at a time.

Make It Fun!

A fun way to practice estimating the time it takes to finish an activity is to guess how much time it will take to finish homework or clean a room, and if they come close to finishing by the estimated time, they may earn a small reward, like 15 extra minutes of screen time or dessert of their choice after dinner.

Another fun activity is to practice coming up with plans quickly by doing timed challenges. The challenges can be simple or complex depending on your child's age, but the important part is to practice planning time.

Let's say you give your children a challenge of creating a way to get from the couch to the front door without touching the floor, but you say that they can stand on a yoga mat. You may give them five minutes to plan and discuss, and then 10 minutes to carry out their plan.

After they either succeed or fail, have a debriefing and ask if there were any unexpected problems that they encountered. You can then discuss questions that are typical in the planning process, like, "What are we going to need?" "What's the most difficult part of this problem?" or "What could keep us from succeeding?" When you normalize these kinds of time management questions and planning through play, kids can more easily apply them to less-fun tasks like homework and chores.

Pro Tip

Children with ADHD and executive functioning skill deficits are unlikely to let you know when or how they are wasting time. As parents, we must sometimes play detective and try to keep an eye out for time wasters.

If your 6-year-old with ADHD seems to be on time in the morning, *until* she goes into her room to put her clothes on, you can assume that something in her room is a distraction. By discussing it with her, she can gain some awareness of what distracts her while she is getting ready for school.

You can then come up with a plan together about how she can stay on task in the morning. Maybe it means agreeing to remove the distracting item from the room and putting it somewhere out of sight until after school. If your child is constantly reading books when she needs to be getting ready, you might just move the books from her room to a common area of the house. Alternatively, you can put a clock directly above the books, so you provide an opportunity for your child to think about time before engaging in that activity. It's in your power to set up the environment to support your child's needs!

Building Resilience

Children with ADHD and executive functioning difficulties may lack resilience, or the ability to adapt to new and difficult situations. The development of resilience is not fixed; there is no true timetable or age in which this skill is necessarily developed. Unlike the skills mentioned in earlier chapters, resilience is more dependent on social and cultural influences. That means you may have more power to influence your child's resilience than other executive functioning skills. In this chapter, you'll get tips on how to foster resilience in your child by encouraging a growth mindset and even normalizing failure as part of the learning process. We'll explore how you can help kids face up to discomfort and challenges they will encounter in life.

Set Them Up for Success

Every childhood is filled with mistakes. Your child may fall off their bike, skin their knee, or fail a big test. The ability to not just recover, but to also learn from these mistakes, is one of the most important skills that you can help your child develop on their way to becoming an independent adult. After all, when they learn to handle and get past the relatively smaller disappointments and hurts of childhood, they'll be far better equipped to deal with the bigger disappointments and hurts of adulthood. In this section, you will learn some general strategies to help develop resilience in your child.

Encourage Autonomy

There is a golden rule that many play therapists embrace: "Never do for a child what they can do for themselves." To raise a resilient child requires some allowance for independence and autonomy. It can be difficult for parents whose children may seem impulsive and need more redirection due to executive functioning issues. But it is imperative, especially for kids with executive functioning weaknesses, to expand their areas of competence so they can feel more in control and confident in their own ability to respond to failure.

This is not as easy as it sounds, of course. If we push a child with ADHD or executive functioning issues to do things they simply are not capable of doing, then we are setting them up for failure and gut punches to their self-esteem. But if we do not push them enough to challenge themselves, then they are not building independence. Tricky, right? Well, to get around this, we can find areas of competence in their lives and push them to do "just a little more" in those areas.

For example, let's say that your 10-year-old daughter with ADHD is good at getting herself ready in the morning. You have practiced the morning routine enough that she has it down. You can then ask her for help getting her 5-year-old sister ready on time. Or if she likes to make breakfast in the morning, you can ask her to make a menu of other things that she would like to try to prepare. When your 5-year-old son asks you to tie his shoes or do something else that you know he has mastered, you can simply say, "That's something you can do." That kind of statement sets the expectation that he can do things for himself and affirms his ability to do things for himself at the same time.

"Helicopter parents," or parents who needlessly solve their children's problems to help them avoid discomfort, can lead to the development of a learned helplessness, or a habit of allowing others to do things for them that they can easily do themselves. Although children with ADHD or executive functioning deficits will need help staying on task or developing strategies to control their impulses, it's important to balance that with steps, and sometimes a push, toward independence.

Connect Emotionally

In a 2015 paper from the National Scientific Council on the Developing Child, it was found that children who do well despite serious hardship have at least one stable and committed relationship with a supportive adult. This finding suggests that resilience requires relationships and not just rugged individualism.

It is vital for parents to model resilience and to find times to connect with our children in good times and bad. When we are calm, patient, and determined, they can learn from that model. And when we make time to be available to our children to talk things through or come up with solutions together, we are forging a lasting connection that will be very valuable in the long term. With many parents busy with work and daily commitments, it is understandably difficult to be consistent with this bonding time, but having a time set aside to spend with your child without expectations is so important to developing this connection.

When you get to this time, make it nonjudgmental and even without an agenda. The sole purpose is to connect emotionally. By giving the child support and praise when they succeed, you are making yourself a person they want to share with. By providing empathy and understanding when they fail, you are normalizing their feelings in the moment. By knowing that you understand how they feel, the child can recover more quickly and stay away from exaggerating the importance of their failure.

And, as mentioned previously, encouragement is a focus on the process and not the result. It's more like, "Maybe you didn't make the team, but you practiced so hard, and you should be proud that you keep practicing." By encouraging your child's effort in the moment, you are giving them the message that their failure in the moment is not final and that their effort is what really counts.

Connecting with a child with ADHD or executive functioning issues can be difficult. They may not see that you are trying to connect with them and be frustrated that they are being asked to leave an activity that excites them. Don't take their resistance personally. Remember, they may not see the big picture, but it is important that you do.

If they resist connecting with you because they are busy with their friends at the moment or forgot some homework and will not be able to make the time you set aside to connect with them, remember that they are not ignoring your attempts to connect—they are just prioritizing the moment they are in, which is typical for children with ADHD and executive functioning deficits, and even kids in general. You'll probably find the best connections can be made when other activities are not winning their attention—bedtime and car rides may be choice settings.

Consider exploring the subject of their day by asking them about the roses (good moments/events) and thorns (not-so-good moments/events) in their day. From these chats, you can effectively cover all the bases of support, praise, empathy, and understanding!

Instill a Growth Mindset

Over 30 years ago, psychologist and researcher Dr. Carol Dweck and her colleagues coined the terms "growth mindset" and "fixed mindset" to describe children's underlying beliefs about learning.

If a child believed that they could learn, grow, and get smarter, then they had a growth mindset, and as such, would put in more effort and be better able to handle difficulty. On the other hand, a child with a fixed mindset believes that they cannot improve, and as a result, they respond more negatively to difficulties in their life. A child's belief in their own capacity for growth was found to lead to more resilient behavior.

Today, a child's ability to subscribe to a growth mindset is still shown to dramatically affect a child's potential for resilience. The good news is a growth mindset can be taught through self-reflection and reframing thoughts.

STOP LABELING

In our day-to-day lives, we are inundated with feedback confirming a fixed mindset, despite scientific evidence showing that our brains do grow and change. A young 4-year-old who is having trouble adjusting to a preschool class might be labeled a "bad boy" by his teacher. The 10-year-old who likes to make jokes in class to distract from the fact that he is having difficulty learning how to conjugate verbs is labeled "the class clown." And the 12-year-old girl who tried a cigarette due to peer pressure is now called a "troublemaker." These labels promote a fixed mindset in these misjudged children.

To promote a growth mindset in your child, you can do your best to avoid labeling your children and avoid labels in general, but also watch out for how they get labeled by others or even label themselves.

Try to help them see the whole picture of a situation. If they say they feel "stupid," you can talk about the fact that everyone has natural abilities, strengths, and weaknesses, and with practice, weaknesses can be strengthened upon. It helps model flexible thinking and a growth mindset. And instead of saying, "You are a bad influence on your sisters," you can say, "Your choices really affect your sisters, because they look up to you so much." By watching out for damaging labels and focusing on your child's choices, you help them understand that they can make a different choice in the future so they aren't "stuck." Growth is possible and a process.

TALK ABOUT THE BRAIN

Another good strategy is to teach your children about how their brains grow. For the child with ADHD, this is especially powerful. For example, you can teach your child with ADHD that their brains are constantly growing—up until they are 25 years old! They may be fascinated to learn that as many as 50 percent of people diagnosed with ADHD as children do not have ADHD as adults. Many children with executive functioning difficulties may assume that they will always be the way they are and will always be behind their peers. It is crucial to remind them that their brains develop in their own time, and they can catch up to their peers.

FOCUS ON EFFORT

Another enemy of the growth mindset is a preoccupation with winning and success. Although many children with ADHD can be competitive and thrive in sports, robotics teams, or family game nights, focusing on the result of competition, rather than the fun of the game, can lead to a fixed mindset. Instead of focusing on winning and losing, you can place emphasis on growth. For example, if your 8-year-old son becomes upset because he didn't win during family game night, instead of saying, "You'll win next time," try praising his effort, good answers, and strategies, and how those skills are important for his life.

THE POWER OF THE WORD "YET"

The most powerful word in the English language is "yet." It can turn a failure into a potential for hope. Let's say your 5-year-old son says, "I can't ride a bike." That is a pretty defeating statement. If you can gently redirect him by saying, "You can't ride a bike *yet*," this small word infuses hope and potential for learning something new. Find opportunities in daily life to model the word "yet." It's a simple way to let your children know that failure is just part of the process of growing and getting better. Before you know it, your child might beat you to it, saying, "Yeah, I know—*yet!*"

Boosting Resilience

There are a few parent traps that can interfere with development of independence in their children. Here you'll learn to recognize common assumptions and thinking patterns that cause children with ADHD to give up quickly, and strategies for how you can help them combat those negative thoughts.

Support Flexible Thinking

According to the previously mentioned study cited in the *Harvard Health Letter*, one of the most promising ways to strengthen resilience and adaptability in children is to develop cognitive flexibility. This is the skill of being able to switch between two different concepts or think about more than one perspective on a situation simultaneously. Cognitive flexibility may be difficult for children with executive functioning issues, but there are a few ways you can work on that skill with your children.

One simple way to boost cognitive flexibility is to provide your child with creative outlets to express themselves. For every competitive or "win-or-lose" activity like sports that your child belongs to, try to have at least one outlet at home or in a group setting that is not focused on winning or losing. It may be a community art class or creative DIY activities to engage artistic thought in your children. You can then have conversations that explore the deeper meaning behind their art without expecting a right or wrong answer. It can help encourage flexible thinking and a growth mindset in your child.

Another way to encourage cognitive flexibility is to allow for open interpretations of events. For example, if your 5-year-old says that they think the sun is a big, hot ball of cheese, instead of shooting them down and telling them how cheddar would freeze in space, you can simply ask, "Why do you think that?" Asking this encourages them to explain their thought process.

If your 11-year-old son says that he thinks a certain basketball team will win the NBA championship, instead of giving your perspective and telling them that they are dead wrong, ask how they came to that theory. If they get into the habit of explaining their reasons behind a thought, they will become more critical of their own thought process. This in turn leads to more cognitive flexibility, because it demands self-evaluation.

By encouraging thoughtful explanations from your children, you are showing respect for different perspectives, which is also important for fostering a growth mindset.

Embrace Failure

Like many children in the 1980s, I grew up in the age of self-esteem. Our parents, counselors, and teachers filled our heads with well-meaning external validation, thinking that positive words would lead to positive self-esteem and achievement. A book called *The Social Importance of Self-Esteem*, penned by several professors at the University of California, helped ignite the fire of the self-esteem movement. Research in this book was misinterpreted in the media, which led to the mistaken belief that if we filled children with positive affirmations of their greatness, they would feel more empowered to achieve more.

In reality, the results from the study were not as overwhelmingly positive as the media and some self-esteem gurus of the time reported. There were some positive correlations, but in other areas their findings were more mixed. Many ignored the fact that a child must first believe that they are capable and competent before they can develop appropriate self-esteem. They must experience success and failure before they can truly believe in themselves.

Although praise often comes from a well-intentioned place, it's important to prioritize competency over confidence. This means providing opportunities to build on what kids can do by trying something more. But children with ADHD and executive functioning issues need more help, so how do you know when to help and when to allow them to try something new and potentially fail?

The most effective parents of children that I work with seem to have appropriate mental boundaries and are not afraid of their child failing. These parents do not take their children's issues as a personal failure, and they are more focused on their child's strengths and solutions to problems rather than their weaknesses and the magnitude of their problems—indeed, these parents have a growth mindset.

A parent's fear of failure with a child with ADHD or executive functioning issues can be particularly harmful. It can lead to feelings of pressure on the child because the child will internalize the pressure from their parents, and they will inevitably make mistakes and feel guilty. In time, it may lead to resentment and anger in both the child and the parent. Failure is an important part of a healthy development process for all children, not just those with ADHD and executive functioning deficits. If you notice that you struggle with your child's failure, and you take these on personally or consistently fear the worst-case scenario, it may help you to find a sounding board to talk through these fears. This could be your partner, a friend, or a therapist. By dealing with your fear, you can gain a healthier perspective and help your child build resilience through failure.

Challenge the Thought, Affirm the Feeling

Many children who lack resilience have likely developed some maladaptive thought patterns over the years. In times of failure, these thoughts pop up automatically. For example, they may label themselves as "a loser." They may think of the worst-case scenario and give up prematurely. They may get stuck on one difficult problem on a test and not be able to move on, because they strive for a perfect score every time. These kinds of examples show a lack of flexibility and too much focus on problems rather than solutions.

One helpful mantra for parents is "Challenge the thought but affirm the feeling." This mantra means that you can disagree with your child's negative assumption about themselves while also empathizing with what they are feeling. Their perception of the situation and their emotional experience can be viewed as separate. For example, let's say your 10-year-old daughter often gives up at the first sign of any failure. After she forgot her homework binder for the second time that week, she says, "I am so stupid! I always forget things!" Your instinct as a parent may be to immediately jump in and say, "No, you're not!" But that removes her from discomfort without creating an opportunity to build resilience. Instead, you can use the following steps to respond in a healthier way:

EMPATHIZE WITH THEIR CORE EXPERIENCE – In this example, you might say, "I used to forget my keys all the time. Forgetting things feels so frustrating. It doesn't make sense that we forget some important things. But I do not think you're stupid." Note how this response validates what they're feeling without agreeing with their statement.

REFRAME THE SITUATION – After empathizing with their feelings, follow up with, "Is there any other way to look at this situation?" If they struggle to reframe the situation, help them by adding your perspective: "I think another way of looking at it is that you are really busy, so your brain sometimes forgets things. Many smart people forget things."

PROBLEM-SOLVE – Once your child is ready to brainstorm a solution without feeling defensive, ask, "Since you've struggled this week with remembering, what do you think we can do to remember next time?"

This way of engaging is a great opportunity to practice resilience because it introduces an opportunity to think in a more flexible way and problem-solve—and that's key to the growth mindset we talked about!

School Support

Children may spend up to 15,000 hours of their lives in school. In all those hours, there are bound to be many opportunities for failure and the development of a resilient mindset. Many schools focus on addressing a child's deficits, but some teachers also do a great job of playing to a child's strengths. This approach focuses on boosting competency in the classroom.

One of my clients, a 7-year-old boy diagnosed with ADHD and disruptive mood dysregulation disorder, struggled with controlling his emotions, specifically when he was asked to do any task that he hadn't completely mastered. For him, learning new things in class was a challenge.

His teacher noticed early on in the school year that the child was interested in the pet hamster in the room and knew a lot about animals, so she gave the child the special responsibility of feeding the hamster daily. The child reported to the class weekly about the hamster's behavior, weight, and facts regarding hamsters in general.

Soon after taking on this responsibility, his attitude toward school shifted. He still had some negative thoughts about his performance, but they were not so absolute. He saw himself as a valuable member of his classroom and began to work more intently on handling difficulty and managing his emotions. By the end of the year, his grades improved, and his parents reported that he was taking on challenges they never thought he would be able to in the past.

Find ways to leverage your child's strengths and interests, even if you feel that they don't directly connect to school performance. Doing so can go a long way in creating a more resilient and positive attitude in your child.

What to Avoid

When it comes to resilience, many parents fall into the role of cheerleader or helicopter parent and have difficulty letting kids feel any discomfort. Some might fall into the other end of the spectrum to become an authoritarian parent who doesn't attend to what their child feels in the moment. Neither extreme is ideal, but both types of parenting neglect the fact that kids must be taught basic executive functioning skills to handle adversity effectively.

Many parents treat adversity as a character lesson rather than an opportunity to help their child develop a skill. If you are telling your child to "pull themselves up by their bootstraps," but they cannot reach their bootstraps, this approach is doing them more harm than good. Resilience is a byproduct of executive functioning development.

There's nothing to be gained by lecturing a child about their mindset or giving them advice on how to view a difficult subject if they don't have the skills to tackle the problem. For example, if your 12-year-old child is giving up because she's overwhelmed that she has a big school project due later in the week and doesn't know where to start, neither positive affirmations nor tough love will help if her brain can't solve the problem in the moment. This child may need your help creating a plan and solving a problem first, before the character-building "bootstrap" talk.

Make It Fun!

A fun way to build resilience as a family is to come up with a "resilient hero" and report every week on a famous pop star, athlete, or fictional character who showed resilience in the face of difficulty.

It's nearly impossible to find a hero in literature, sports, or movies who hasn't faced some adversity. By helping your child realize that adversity is universal and not just unique to them, it may be easier for them to handle. If your child likes a specific book series, movie franchise, or team sport, you can ask them to report on a different person or character every week within that series or team. Here are some questions you can use to guide them:

→ "What was this person/character's biggest challenge?"
→ "What was their mindset or what did they tell themselves to get through that difficulty?"
→ "How did their difficulty help them grow?"

These types of questions not only help normalize conflicts in life, but they also encourage kids to develop a growth mindset during difficult times.

Pro Tip

Children with ADHD and executive functioning issues may have difficulty with certain skills, but they are very keen observers. Parents can be extremely effective teachers by modeling a growth mindset and resilient behavior. Try to catch yourself when you are exaggerating problems or over-reacting to setbacks due to stress. Be aware of when you are being overly critical because you worry about your child's future. Your behavior is key to helping your child see what a resilient mindset looks like in daily life. You have the ability to influence this critical skill, which will serve them in daily life now and throughout their life.

CLOSING THOUGHTS

Parenting a child with ADHD or executive functioning issues comes with many challenges. But the number-one predictor of later success for a child with executive functioning difficulties is parental involvement.

By reading this book, you've taken the first step in an important journey to embracing your child and their unique needs. I hope this book has given you a deeper understanding of children with executive functioning difficulties and some concrete tools to support them.

Like your children, you are in the process of growing as a parent. Just as you may show grace to your child if they leave their homework on the kitchen table, I encourage you to be kind to yourself if you happen to temporarily lose sight of bigger parenting goals. We are all a work in progress, and that is a great thing!

Finally, my hope is that you can share what you have learned about ADHD and executive functioning to help other parents who may be struggling. As more and more parents share knowledge and resources with one another, we will learn more about how different children think and grow differently. In time, more and more people will see that a child whose brain may be wired a little differently has just as much potential for success and a fulfilling life as anybody else.

RESOURCES

Breathe, Think, Do with Sesame
CommonSenseMedia.org/app-reviews/breathe
-think-do-with-sesame

CBT Thought Diary
CBTThoughtDiary.com

Mindful Family
Mindful-App.com/#Home

Sleep Meditations for Kids
Apps.Apple.com/us/app/sleep-meditations-for-kids
/id549414156

Smiling Mind
SmilingMind.com.au/smiling-mind-app

Websites

ADDitude Magazine
ADDitudemag.com

CHADD (Children and Adults with Attention-Deficit
/Hyperactivity Disorder)
CHADD.org

Healthy Children: Resources on ADHD
HealthyChildren.org/English/health-issues/conditions/adhd

Books

ADHD 2.0: New Science and Essential Stategies for Thriving with Distraction—from Childhood through Adulthood by Edward M. Hallowell and John J. Ratey

From Chaos to Calm: Effective Parenting for Challenging Children with ADHD and Other Behavioral Problems by Janet E. Heininger and Sharon K. Weiss

Growth Mindset Activities for Kids: 55 Exercises to Embrace Learning and Overcome Challenges by Esther Pia Cordova

Simon Says Pay Attention: Help for Children with ADHD by Daniel Yeager and Marcie Yeager

Thriving with ADHD Workbook for Kids: 60 Fun Activities to Help Children Self-Regulate, Focus, and Succeed by Kelli Miller, LCSW, MSW

REFERENCES

Barkley, Russell A. "Advances in Management of ADHD: Evidence-Based Medications and Psychosocial Treatment." Virtual training presentation at PESI, Eau Claire, Wisconsin, 2018.

Bertin, Mark. *The Family ADHD Solution: A Scientific Approach to Maximizing Your Child's Attention and Minimizing Parental Stress.* New York: St. Martin's Press, 2011.

Best, John R., and Patricia H. Miller. "A Developmental Perspective on Executive Functioning." *Child Development* 81, no. 6 (November–December 2010): 1641–1660. doi: 10.1111/j.1467-8624.2010.01499.x.

Bhandari, Smitha. "The Link between Depression and ADHD." WebMD. Accessed September 6, 2020. WebMD.com/add-adhd/depression-adhd-link.

Bhandari, Smitha. "Time Management for Teens and Tweens With ADHD." WebMD. Accessed September 5, 2020. WebMD.com/add-adhd/childhood-adhd/teens-tweens-adhd-time-management.

Boring, Melinda. "You Would Forget Your Head . . ." *ADDitude.* Accessed July 28, 2020. ADDitudemag.com/improve-memory-adhd-child.

Buzanko, Caroline. "The Key to Cultivating ADHD Emotional Regulation? Cultivating, Gratitude, Pride & Compassion." *ADDitude.* Accessed August 2, 2020. ADDitudemag.com /emotional-regulation-adhd-kids-strategies.

Centers for Disease Control and Prevention. "ADHD in the Classroom: Helping Children Succeed in School." Accessed August 30, 2020. CDC.gov/ncbddd/adhd/school-success.html.

Chang, L., D. Schwartz, K.A. Dodge, and C. Mcbride-Chang. "Harsh Parenting in Relation to Child Emotion Regulation and Aggression." *Journal of Family Psychology* 17, no. 4 (2003): 598–606. doi: 10.1037/0893-3200.17.4.598.

Danneman, Ilana. "How to Calm a Sensory Seeking Child." *ADDitude.* Accessed September 19, 2020. ADDitudemag.com /sensory-break-ideas.

The Derek Bok Center for Teaching and Learning. "How Memory Works." Accessed July 29, 2020. BokCenter.Harvard .edu/how-memory-works.

Dewar, Gwen. "Working Memory in Children: What You Need to Know." Parenting Science. Accessed August 1, 2020. ParentingScience.com/working-memory.html.

Dingman, Marc. "Know Your Brain: Orbitofrontal Cortex." Neuroscientifically Challenged. Published May 13, 2015.

Doran, G. T. "There's a S.M.A.R.T. Way to Write Management's Goals and Objectives." *Management Review* 70, no. 11 (1981): 35–36.

Duke Estroff, Sharon. "The Age-by-Age Guide to Teaching Kids Time Management." Scholastic. Accessed September 5, 2020.

Eanes, Rebecca. "25 Ways to Calm an Upset Child." *Creative Child*. Accessed September 19, 2020. CreativeChild.com /articles/view/25-ways-to-calm-an-upset-child/1#page_title.

El-Naggar, Nahed Saied, Manal Hassan Abo-Elmagd, and Hanan Ibrahim Ahmed. "Effect of Applying Play Therapy on Children with Attention Deficit Hyperactivity Disorder." *Journal of Nursing Education and Practice* 7, no. 5 (January 2017): 104–119. doi: 10.5430/jnep.v7n5p104.

Firestone, Lisa. "Tips for Helping Kids Handle Their Emotions." *Psychology Today*. Published January 18, 2012. PsychologyToday.com/us/blog/compassion-matters/201201 /tips-helping-kids-handle-their-emotions.

Fischer, Anna V., and Karrie E. Godwin. "Heavily Decorated Classrooms Disrupt Attention and Learning in Young Children." Association for Psychological Science. Published May 27, 2014. PsychologicalScience.org/news/releases /heavily-decorated-classrooms-disrupt-attention-and -learning-in-young-children.html.

Flippin, Royce. "Why Is My Child So Angry and Defiant? An Overview of Oppositional Defiant Disorder." *ADDitude*. Accessed July 26, 2020. ADDitudemag.com/parenting-a-defiant -adhd-child.

Gemm Learning. "Symptoms of Working Memory Issues: Working Memory Dysfunction Signs by Age and Type." Accessed August 2, 2020. GemmLearning.com/can-help /working-memory/symptoms.

Godman, Heidi. "Regular Exercise Changes the Brain to Improve Memory, Thinking Skills." *Harvard Health Letter*.

Accessed August 3, 2020. Harvard Health Publishing. Health.Harvard.edu/blog/regular-exercise-changes-brain -improve-memory-thinking-skills-201404097110.

Goldrich, Cindy. "Executive Function: ADHD and Stress in the Classroom." Virtual training presentation at PESI, Eau Claire, Wisconsin, 2017.

Greene, Ross W. *The Explosive Child: A New Approach for Understanding and Parenting Easily Frustrated, Chronically Inflexible Children.* 5th ed. New York: HarperCollins, 2014.

Hallowell, Edward M., and John J. Ratey. *Driven to Distraction: Recognizing and Coping with Attention Deficit Disorder from Childhood through Adulthood.* New York: Simon & Schuster, 2011.

Harvard Health Publishing. "Ramp up Your Resilience!" Harvard Health, November 17, 2017. Health.Harvard.edu /mind-and-mood/ramp-up-your-resilience.

Haughey, Duncan. "A Brief History of SMART Goals." Project Smart. Published December 13, 2014.

Jacobs, Denise. "Breaking the Perfectionism–Procrastination Infinite Loop." Web Standards Sherpa. Published May 20, 2014. WebStandardsSherpa.com/reviews/breaking-the -perfectionism-procrastination-infinite-loop.html.

Klemm, William R. "Training Working Memory: Why and How." *Psychology Today.* Published March 26, 2012. Psychology Today.com/us/blog/memory-medic/201203/training-working -memory-why-and-how.

Klingberg, Torkel, Elisabeth Fernell, Pernille J. Olesen, et al. "Computerized Training of Working Memory in Children with

ADHD—A Randomized, Controlled Trial." *Journal of the American Academy of Child and Adolescent Psychiatry* 44, no. 2 (February 2005): 177–186. doi: 10.1097/00004583-200502000-00010.

Lally, Phillipa, Cornelia H.M. van Jaarsveld, Henry W.W. Potts, and Jane Wardle. "How Habits Are Formed: Modelling Habit Formation in the Real World." *European Journal of Social Psychology* 40, no. 6 (October 2010): 998–1009. doi.org/10.1002/ejsp.674.

Low, Keath. "Improving Your Working Memory with ADD." Very Well Mind. Published February 15, 2020. verywellmind.com/add-and-working-memory-20796.

Markham, Laura. "8 Steps to Help Your Child Develop Self-Control." *Psychology Today.* Published June 17, 2015. PsychologyToday.com/us/blog/peaceful-parents-happy-kids/201506/8-steps-help-your-child-develop-self-control.

McKay, Matthew. *When Anger Hurts Your Kids: a Parent's Guide.* Oakland, California: New Harbinger Publications, 1996.

Melbourne Child Psychology & School Psychology Services. "The Impact on Working Memory Difficulties on Learning." Accessed August 2, 2020. MelbourneChildPsychology.com.au/blog/impact-working-memory-difficulties-learning.

Mindset Works. "Dr. Dweck's Research Into Growth Mindset Changed Education Forever." Accessed August 13, 2020. mindsetworks.com/science.

Mokrova, Irina, Marion O'Brien, Susan Calkins, and Susan Keane. "Parental ADHD Symptomology and Ineffective

Parenting: The Connecting Link of Home Chaos." *Parenting: Science and Practice* 10, no. 2 (April 2010): 119–135. doi: 10.1080/15295190903212844.

National Scientific Council on the Developing Child. "Supportive Relationships and Active Skill-Building Strengthen the Foundations of Resilience (PDF)." Working Paper 13. Published 2015. 46y5eh11fhgw3ve3ytpwxt9r-wpengine.netdna-ssl.com/wp-content/uploads/2015/05/The-Science-of-Resilience2.pdf.

Nowell, David, PhD. "Changing the ADHD Brain: Moving Beyond Medication." DVD. Eau Claire, WI: PESI Inc., 2016

Oppong, Thomas. "The Time of Day Has a Significant Effect on Your Productivity." The Ladders. Published May 20, 2019. TheLadders.com/career-advice/the-time-of-day-has-a-significant-effect-on-your-productivity.

Parker-Pope, Tara. "A 'Dose of Nature' for Attention Problems." *Well* (blog). Published October 17, 2008. Well.Blogs.NYTimes.com/2008/10/17/a-dose-of-nature-for-attention-problems.

Ratey, John J. *Spark: The Revolutionary New Science of Exercise and the Brain*. New York: Little, Brown, 2008.

The Redbooth Team. "Everybody's Working for the Weekend, but When Do You Actually Get Work Done?" Published November 15, 2017. Redbooth.com/blog/your-most-productive-time.

Rotz, Roland, and Sarah D. Wright. "The Body–Brain Connection: How Fidgeting Sharpens Focus." *ADDitude*. Accessed September 1, 2020. ADDitudemag.com/focus-factors.

Saarni, Carolyn. "Emotional Development in Childhood." Encyclopedia on Early Childhood Development. Published

September 2011. Child-Encyclopedia.com/emotions
/according-experts/emotional-development-childhood.

Schmitt, Barton D. "Attention Deficit/Hyperactivity Disorder
(ADHD): How to Help Your Child." Summit Medical Group.
Accessed August 15, 2020. SummitMedicalGroup.com/library
/pediatric_health/pa-hhgbeh_attention.

Schmitt, Barton D. *My Child Is Sick!: Expert Advice for Managing Common Illnesses and Injuries.* Elk Grove Village, Illinois:
American Academy of Pediatrics, 2017.

Schultz, Jerome. "I Am What I Choose to Become." *ADDitude.*
Updated July 15, 2020. ADDitudemag.com/teaching-resilience
-to-adhd-children.

Sibley, Margaret H. *Parent–Teen Therapy for Executive Function
Deficits and ADHD: Building Skills and Motivation.* New York:
Guilford Press, 2017.

Siegel, Daniel J. *The Whole-Brain Child: 12 Revolutionary Strategies to Nurture Your Child's Developing Mind.* New York: Bantam
Books, 2011.

Sosic-Vasec, Zrinka, Julia Kröner, Sibylle Schneider, Nenad
Vasic, Manfred Spitzer, and Judith Streb. "The Association
between Parenting Behavior and Executive Functioning in
Children and Young Adolescents." Frontiers in Psychology.
Published March 30, 2017. doi.org/10.3389/fpsyg.2017.00472.

Storr, Will. "'It was Quasi-religious': The Great Self-esteem
Con." *The Guardian.* Published June 3, 2017. TheGuardian.
com/lifeandstyle/2017/jun/03/quasi-religious-great-self
-esteem-con.

Sylwester, Robert, and Joo-Yun Cho. "What Brain Research Says about Paying Attention." *Students at Risk* 50, no. 4 (December 1992/January 1993): 71–75.

Tahnk, Jeana Lee. "6 Meditation and Mindfulness Apps for Kids." *Parents.* Published February 19, 2019. Parents.com /health/healthy-happy-kids/5-mindfulness-and-meditation -apps-for-kids.

Taylor, Andrea Faber, and Frances E. Kuo. "Children with Attention Deficits Concentrate Better after Walk in the Park." *Journal of Attention Disorders* 12, no. 5 (August 5, 2008): 402–409. doi: 10.1177/1087054708323000.

Tocino-Smith, Juliette. "Teaching Resilience in Schools and Fostering Resilient Learners." PositivePsychology.com. Published January 9, 2020. PositivePsychology.com/teaching -resilience.

van der Oord, Saskia, Susan M. Bögels, and Dorreke Peijnen- burg. "The Effectiveness of Mindfulness Training for Children with ADHD and Mindful Parenting for their Parents." *Journal of Child and Family Studies* 21, no. 1 (February 2011): 139–147. doi: 10.1007/s10826-011-9457-0.

Vassar, Gerry. "How Does a Parent's Anger Impact His or Her Child?" Lakeside. Published March 10, 2011. LakesideLink. com/blog/lakeside/how-does-a-parents-anger-impact-his -or-her-child.

Walg, Marco, Gerhard Hapfelmeier, Daniel El-Wahsch, and Helmut Pior. "The Faster Internal Clock in ADHD Is Related to Lower Processing Speed: WISC-IV Profile Analyses and Time Estimation Tasks Facilitate the Distinction between Real

ADHD and Pseudo-ADHD." *European Child & Adolescent Psychiatry* 26, no. 10 (October 2017): 1177–1186. doi: 10.1007 /s00787-017-0971-5.

Weitbrecht, Walter-Uwe, H. Bärwolff, A. Lischke, and S. Jünger. "Effect of Light Color Temperature on Human Concentration and Creativity." *Fortschritte der Neurologie Psychiatrie* 83, no. 6 (June 2015): 344–348. doi: 10.1055 /s-0035-1553051.

Yeager, D., and M. Yeager. *Simon Says Pay Attention: Help for Children with ADHD.* 3rd ed. Golden Path Games, 2016.

Young-Eisendrath, Polly. *The Self-Esteem Trap: Raising Confident and Compassionate Kids in the Age of Self-Importance.* New York: Hachette Book Group, 2008.

Zentall, Sydney S. *ADHD and Education: Foundations, Characteristics, Methods, and Collaboration.* Upper Saddle River, NJ: Pearson/Merrill Prentice Hall, 2006.

Zohar, Ada H., Lior Pesah Shimone, and Meirav Hen. "Active and Passive Procrastination in Terms of Temperament and Character." *PeerJ* 7, no. 6988 (May 29, 2019). doi: 10.7717 /peerj.6988. eCollection 2019.

INDEX

T

Thoughts, negative, 31–32
Thought Villains, 86–88
Time management
    about, 8–9, 147
    estimating time, 152–153
    games, 159–160
    long-term task planning, 150–152
    measuring time, 155
    minimizing distractions, 160
    mistakes to avoid, 158–159
    parental modeling, 35–36
    and planning abilities, 148–149
    and procrastination, 153–157
    school support for, 157–158

W

When Anger Hurts Your Kids
    (McKay), 80
Working memory
    about, 6–7, 101–102
    allowing time for tasks, 105–106

    exercise and, 103–104
    games, 113
    "get in your own way"
        strategies, 102–103
    information retrieval, 106–110
    mistakes to avoid, 112
    parental, 32–33
    school support for, 110–112
    sensory cues, 104–105
    visualization techniques, 113–114

Y

Young-Eisendrath, Polly, 124

Z

Zentall, Sydney S., 141

ABOUT THE AUTHOR

ZAC GRISHAM, MS, LPC-S, ADHD-CCSP, is a licensed professional counselor supervisor and owner of Clear View Counseling in Dallas, Texas. He is a certified ADHD specialist who brings his own personal ADHD diagnosis and firsthand experience navigating executive functioning deficits to inform his practice. A former elementary school teacher and member of the Academy of Cognitive Therapy, Zac has been named a "Mom Approved" therapist by *DFW Child* magazine from 2014 to 2020. He continues to work closely with individuals and families dealing with a diagnosis of ADHD through counseling and parent training.